TOTAL YOUTH MINISTRY

Community Life

MINISTRY RESOURCES FOR   **Youth Leadership Development**

Pastoral Care

Prayer and Worship

Evangelization

Justice and Service

Pray It! Study It! Live It!™ resources offer a holistic approach
to learning, living, and passing on the Catholic faith.

The Total Faith™ Initiative

Total Catechesis
Catechetical Sessions on Christian Morality
Catechetical Sessions on Christian Prayer
Catechetical Sessions on Liturgy and the Sacraments
Catechetical Sessions on the Creed

Total Youth Ministry
Ministry Resources for Community Life
Ministry Resources for Evangelization
Ministry Resources for Justice and Service
Ministry Resources for Pastoral Care
Ministry Resources for Prayer and Worship
Ministry Resources for Youth Leadership Development

Total Faith™ Initiative Coordinator's Manual

The Catholic Faith Handbook for Youth

The Catholic Youth Bible™

TOTAL YOUTH MINISTRY

Community Life

MINISTRY RESOURCES FOR **Youth Leadership Development**

Pastoral Care

Prayer and Worship

Evangelization

Justice and Service

Ann Marie Eckert with Maria Sánchez-Keane

Saint Mary's Press™

This book is dedicated to all the leaders who have taught and mentored me, to those whose examples inspire me, and to the young people whom I have had the privilege of walking with during their early leadership years.

—Ann Marie Eckert

 Genuine recycled paper with 10% post-consumer waste. Printed with soy-based ink. 5055401

Contributors

The following authors contributed to this manual:

- Anne Bretzlauf, Omaha, Nebraska—"Jesus on Leadership"
- Kathy Kensinger, Omaha, Nebraska—"Strategies for Parents of Young Leaders" and "Leadership Is Making a Difference for Good"
- Steve Nespor, Omaha, Nebraska—"Giving a Witness Talk"
- Maria Sánchez-Keane, London, Ontario, Canada—"Naming and Claiming Gifts in Self and Others," "Leading Group Discussions," "Negotiating Skills," "Planning Skills," and "Reflective Listening Skills"
- Jennifer Vankat, Omaha, Nebraska—"Jesus on Leadership"
- Julie Vankat, Omaha, Nebraska—"Unexpected Leaders of the Bible" and "Communication Skills"

The following people contributed to this resource by providing ideas, strategies, and activities:

Marie Angele, Omaha, Nebraska

Carol Fischer, Omaha, Nebraska

Barbara Gawlik, Omaha, Nebraska

Debra Kaufman, Omaha, Nebraska

Tom Murray, Omaha, Nebraska

Jennifer Oliva, Omaha, Nebraska

Rita Ramos, Omaha, Nebraska

Shannon Smith, Omaha, Nebraska

Gabrielle Tarr, Omaha, Nebraska

Additional thanks to the youth ministry community in Omaha, Nebraska, for their help in conceiving the contents of this resource.

The publishing team included Laurie Delgatto and Barbara Murray, development editors; Penelope Bonnar and Cheryl Drivdahl, copy editors; Barbara Bartelson, production editor; Cären Yang, art director and designer; Jonathan Thomas Goebel, cover designer; Digital Imagery © PhotoDisc, Inc., cover images; Alan S. Hanson, prepress specialist; Elly Poppe, CD-ROM developer; manufacturing coordinated by the production services department of Saint Mary's Press.

Produced with the assistance of settingPace, LLC, Cincinnati, Ohio.

Ministry resource manuals were developed in collaboration with the Center for Ministry Development. The publishing team included Thomas East, project coordinator, and Cheryl Tholcke, content editor.

Printed in the United States of America

Printing: 9 8 7 6 5 4 3 2

Year: 2012 11 10 09 08 07 06 05 04

ISBN 0-88489-769-9

Contents

Youth and Adults Working Together

Introduction

About Total Youth Ministry

Many youth today are waiting to hear the Good News that is ours as Christ's disciples. Youth in our parishes long to grow spiritually and to belong to their family, Church, and local community in meaningful ways. Parents of youth long to experience Church as supportive of and caring about the same things they care about. They hope the parish will offer ways for youth to be involved and to grow in their faith. Parents want to understand youth ministry so they can support and encourage their child's participation.

Parishes want to know how to include youth and how to pass on faith to a new generation. Parish members want to see youth more involved, and are worried about the challenges that face today's youth. They know that young people need support from their faith community—now more than ever. Parish youth ministry leaders are generous, passionate, and busy people; they make sacrifices so that youth will have a community to belong to and a place to grow. They need ideas and plans for youth ministry activities—and strategies that really work. They are working toward a ministry that goes beyond just gathering groups of young people; they are working toward a ministry that makes connections between youth and the community.

All those voices have something in common—a longing for youth ministry that is inclusive, dynamic, and flexible.

In 1997 the United States Conference of Catholic Bishops (USCCB) published its blueprint for youth ministry in the twenty-first century. *Renewing the Vision: A Framework for Catholic Youth Ministry* challenges youth ministry to focus its efforts in these directions:

- to empower young people to live as disciples of Jesus Christ in our world today
- to draw young people to responsible participation in the life, mission, and work of the Catholic faith community
- to foster the total personal and spiritual growth of each young person

In *Renewing the Vision*, the bishops urge the Church to guide young people toward a life of fullness in Jesus Christ, and to give them the tools that will enable them to live out that fullness as Catholic Christians. To put it simply, the bishops call young people to embrace their faith as they study it, pray it, and live it. The bishops also challenge the faith community to surround young people with love, care, and attention and to include youth throughout the life of the parish.

The Ministry Resource Manuals

The ministry resource manuals of the Total Youth Ministry series address each of the components of youth ministry as outlined in *Renewing the Vision*. The advocacy and catechesis components are woven throughout the ministry resource manuals. You will find the following information in each of the ministry resource manuals:

- a chapter explaining the component, connecting it to Church documents, and identifying practical ideas and resources for implementing the component
- sessions that can stand alone or be combined with others in the series
- numerous strategies, ideas, suggestions, and resources that go beyond a specific gathering

Following is a brief description of each of the manuals:

- *Ministry Resources for Community Life* offers faith communities program resources and strategies to build community among young people and throughout the entire parish. The resource includes nine gathered sessions to help young people get to know one another, themselves, and the meaning of Christian community. It also contains an outline for an ecumenical event to help build community across denominational lines, and it offers practical strategies and ideas to help manage community issues, make the most of community life opportunities, and encourage intergenerational and family relationships.
- *Ministry Resources for Evangelization* offers faith communities tools and program resources to evangelize youth. It offers practical strategies and ideas for outreach to young people and contains twelve gathered sessions to share the Good News. It also includes a retreat to engage young people in becoming or continuing as Jesus' disciples.
- *Ministry Resources for Justice and Service* offers faith communities programs and strategies to engage youth in justice, direct service, and advocacy in faithful, age-appropriate, and proactive ways. This resource contains eight gathered sessions around specific justice issues, an overnight retreat on service to poor people, and two half-day retreats or evening reflections on simplicity and racism.

- At the heart of *Ministry Resources for Pastoral Care* are twelve sessions designed to equip young people with the tools needed to celebrate their holy goodness and navigate some of life's difficult issues. The topics of the sessions include recognizing the goodness in oneself and others, building and maintaining relationships, dealing with tough times, and preparing for the future. The last section of the manual comprises strategies for doing the ongoing work of pastoral care.

- *Ministry Resources for Prayer and Worship* is designed for those who work with and walk with youth in this journey of discipleship. The manual contains three sessions to teach youth to pray and to practice praying in different forms. Eleven communal prayer services are included, which can be used on a variety of occasions throughout the seasons of the year. The manual also contains strategies and resources to help youth communities develop patterns of prayer and to include youth in preparing prayers and liturgies.

- *Ministry Resources for Youth Leadership Development* offers faith communities program resources and strategies to develop youth as leaders within youth ministry programs and the parish. The manual includes four foundational sessions on Christian leadership, ten leadership skill sessions and minisessions, and two sessions to help prepare youth and adults for working together. The manual offers ideas and strategies for creating leadership roles within the parish, inviting youth to leadership, and working with the parents of youth leaders. The plans for implementing sessions and other gathered events are complete, easy to follow, and adaptable to your community.

With the detailed plans provided for the sessions, activities, and strategies in Total Youth Ministry, youth ministry volunteers no longer need to be program designers. By using the Total Youth Ministry resources, you can focus on the important task of finding the leaders who make youth ministry happen. Each session includes an overview, a list of materials, preparation steps, and step-by-step instructions for facilitating a session with confidence. Most sessions also include a variety of ways to extend the theme of the session with prayer, related learning exercises, or follow-through experiences.

An Added Feature: CD-ROMs

Each manual has a CD-ROM that includes the full content of the manual. This feature enables the user to provide handouts and resource materials to adult leaders, parents, and the young people in a variety of delivery methods, such as e-mail, Web site posting, and photocopying. Handouts and resources are provided in printable color versions (which cannot be customized) and in black-and-white versions that you can customize for the particular needs of a group. You will also find hyperlinks to suggested Web sites.

Participant Resources

Much of the material in the ministry resource manuals is designed to work in a complementary way with the contents of *The Catholic Faith Handbook for Youth (CFH)* and *The Catholic Youth Bible (CYB)*.

Ministry Resources for Youth Leadership Development: An Overview

Ministry Resources for Youth Leadership Development offers faith communities program resources and strategies to develop youth as leaders within youth ministry programs and the parish. The manual includes four foundational sessions on Christian leadership, ten sessions and minisessions on leadership skills, and two minisessions to help prepare youth and adults for working together. The manual also offers strategies for using the activities, sessions, and minisessions to create daylong, weekend-long, and yearlong training programs for youth; for creating leadership roles within the parish; for inviting youth to leadership; and for working with the parents of youth leaders.

Manual Contents

Part A: Introductory Article

Part A of *Ministry Resources for Youth Leadership Development* explores the importance of training and mentoring youth as leaders, creating opportunities across the parish ministries for youth to be involved in leadership, and thinking broadly about who is a leader and what leadership entails.

Part B: Strategies

Part B of this manual consists of strategies that adult leaders in a parish can use to organize the activities, sessions, and minisessions from parts C and D into a leadership training program; find and create leadership positions for youth; invite young people into youth leadership roles; and support the parents of young leaders. Each strategy contains information to help leaders grow in their understanding of the issue, followed by practical ideas that can be implemented within the parish.

Chapter 2: Using This Manual to Develop Youth Leadership
• This strategy lists the sessions that can be used to build an understanding of leadership, the sessions that can be combined for strong skill building,

and the sessions that can help youth and adults learn how to work together effectively.

Chapter 3: Creating Parish Leadership Positions for Youth
- This chapter is designed to help adult leaders work within parish structures to create leadership opportunities for youth. Included are ways to help parish staff, organizations, and ministries understand the need for youth leadership. Also provided are resources to help parish ministries and organizations create leadership roles for youth, and suggestions for working with the community and schools to involve youth in leadership.

Chapter 4: Inviting Youth into Leadership
- This chapter looks at ways to invite youth into leadership roles and to form them as leaders. Included are ways to assess young people's interests in leadership roles and to share parish leadership opportunities with them.

Chapter 5: Strategies for Parents of Young Leaders
- This chapter contains ideas for reaching out to the parents of young leaders. Included are suggestions for communicating and meeting with them.

Part C: Leadership Sessions

The youth leadership development sessions include foundational sessions that provide a broad overview of leadership plus a look at scriptural images of leadership. They also include four sessions for training youth in essential leadership skills.

The sessions are about 60 minutes long and are sometimes accompanied by 15- to 30-minute session extensions. They are not sequential, so you may organize them to suit your situation.

Each session begins with a brief overview, a list of expected outcomes, and background reading that may include a list of scriptural connections and *Catholic Youth Bible* article connections. All articles are excerpted from the first edition of the *CYB*. The next element is a suggested schedule, which is to be used as a starting point and modified according to your circumstances. A checklist of required presentation steps includes all materials needed. A complete description of the session procedure is then provided, including all activities, session extensions, prayer experiences, and options and actions.

Study It

Each session can be expanded and customized to meet your schedule and the needs of your group. You may expand the sessions by using additional activities known as session extensions. Musical selections from *Spirit & Song* are provided for your reference. Music resources are available from a variety of music publishers, and a Bible concordance will provide additional citations if you want to add a more substantial scriptural component to a session. *The Saint Mary's Press Essential Bible Concordance* offers a simple, user-friendly index to key words in the Bible. Some sessions provide a list of media resources—such as print, video, and Internet—for more exploration. Family approaches provide follow-up suggestions for family learning, enrichment, celebration, prayer, and service.

Pray It: Prayer Experiences

Each session includes opportunities and suggestions for prayer focused on the session's theme. Prayer forms include guided meditation, shared prayer, music, silence, prayer by young people, reflective reading, and experiences created by the participants. The Pray It component gives the young people an opportunity to bring their insights and concerns to God in prayer. The time frame for prayer experiences varies from 5 to 20 minutes.

Live It: Options and Actions

This manual can be a springboard for connections with other youth ministry experiences. Therefore some of its sessions include additional strategies to support the learning process. Those activities can be used to extend the session, provide good follow-up for the Study It core sessions, and allow for age-appropriate assimilation of the material.

Chapter 6: Leadership Is Making a Difference for Good

- This session helps the young people discover that leadership means much more than just being the up-front person, that it means making a difference for good in the world.

Chapter 7: Jesus on Leadership

- This session explores Jesus as a model for leadership. The participants are invited to reflect on that example, explore the leadership qualities of Jesus, and discover ways that they can follow his example within their own lives.

Chapter 8: Unexpected Leaders of the Bible

- This session uses characters from the Bible to help the participants recognize different styles of leadership and the humanness of the people that God has called through the years.

Chapter 9: Naming and Claiming Gifts in Self and Others

- This session invites the participants to reflect on how God has called them, what gifts they have received, and how they can use those gifts to serve others.

Chapter 10: Communication Skills

- This session helps the participants understand the communication process, including the challenges of trying to communicate effectively.

Chapter 11: Leading Group Discussions

- This session provides the participants with an opportunity to reflect on the skills that make someone an effective group facilitator.

Chapter 12: Negotiating Skills
- This session teaches the participants the skills necessary for negotiating effectively and then allows them to practice those skills.

Chapter 13: Planning Skills
- This session helps the participants think about the steps involved in effective planning. It introduces a program planning process and provides practice on planning with others.

Part D: Minisessions

The minisessions in this section are designed to complement the more in-depth sessions in section C, and can also be used as shorter learning experiences. The sessions are 15 to 70 minutes long.

Chapter 14: Large-Group Communication
- This session teaches the participants how to capture a group's attention, give announcements, and share information in large-group formats.

Chapter 15: Attentive Listening Skills
- This session teaches the participants the importance of listening well using nonverbal attending skills.

Chapter 16: Reflective Listening Skills
- This session provides an overview of the skills necessary to listen reflectively to another person.

Chapter 17: Group Decision-Making Skills
- This session introduces a decision-making process.

Chapter 18: Effective Meeting Skills
- This session introduces the necessary elements of effective meetings, including the important roles of facilitator, timekeeper, and recorder.

Chapter 19: Giving a Witness Talk
- This session provides information and ideas to those who will be sharing their faith through a witness talk. The participants learn what to do to prepare a talk, and reflect on the importance of sharing their faith with others.

Chapter 20: Knowing Youth
- This session helps adults recognize their role in welcoming young people to an organization or ministry, and provides helpful hints for working with youth.

Chapter 21: Knowing Adults
- This session helps young people recognize their role in intergenerational groups and ministries, and open themselves to the ideas and gifts of adults.

Background Material on the CD-ROM

The background piece, "Qualities of Effective Christian Leaders," will help those who are leading chapter 7, "Jesus on Leadership," or any of the leadership sessions. The article describes the qualities that make leaders more effective and the ways that Christians can pull from Jesus' life and example to integrate leadership qualities into their own lives. The article is on the CD-ROM that accompanies the manual so that you can easily distribute it to other leaders.

Handouts and Resources

All the necessary handouts and resources are found at the end of each chapter in the manual. They are also found on the accompanying CD-ROM, in both color and black-and-white versions. The black-and-white materials may be customized to suit your particular needs.

Facilitating the Sessions

Role Models

Through the example of youth ministry leaders (both adults and youth), young people learn what it means to be a Christian leader. It is essential that those in positions of leadership be attentive to the example they are setting, in both words and actions. It is also important that they use the leadership skills they are teaching, during the sessions and throughout the year.

Hospitality and Community Building

Hospitality and community building are significant parts of all youth ministry functions, including leadership team meetings and leadership training sessions. An important aspect of community building is the attitude of those involved in leadership. Leaders, both youth and adults, must build community with those who attend events and programs.

Presentations

In each session, the leaders are asked to make presentations of key concepts and teachings. Ensure that those presentations are effective by practicing them ahead of time, personalizing the materials with the addition of your own stories and examples, familiarizing yourself with the material, and inviting constructive criticism from other leaders. If necessary, do some outside reading or learning about the skills and ideas you will be presenting. The quality of the leadership training young people receive in these sessions will depend, in part, on how well you know the skills yourself and how familiar you are with the material.

Facilitation

The skills of large-group facilitation are important. When working with the young people, the leaders of sessions or activities should have a strong understanding of the entire session and of their role within it. The leaders should be attentive to the time allotted for each activity and to the core purpose of the activity.

Preparing Yourself

Read each session or activity before you facilitate it, then use it creatively to meet the needs of the young people in your group. Knowing your audience will help you determine which activities will work best. Some activities require preparation. Allow yourself adequate time to get ready.

Standard Materials

To save time, consider gathering frequently used materials in bins and storing those bins in a place that is accessible to all staff and volunteer leaders. Here are some recommendations for organizing the bins.

Supply Bin

The following items appear frequently in the materials checklists:

- copies of *The Catholic Youth Bible,* at least one for every two participants
- one copy of *The Catholic Faith Handbook for Youth* for your reference
- masking tape
- washable and permanent markers (thick-line and thin-line)
- pens or pencils
- self-stick notes
- scissors
- newsprint
- glue sticks
- magazines and newspapers
- poster board
- a hole punch
- yarn or string
- foam balls
- blank paper, scrap paper, and notebook paper
- candles and matches
- items to create a prayer space (for example, a colored cloth, a cross, a bowl for water, and a vase for flowers)

Music Bin

Young people often find profound meaning in the music and lyrics of songs, both past and present. Also, the right music can set the appropriate mood for a prayer or an activity. Begin with a small collection of tapes or CDs in a music bin, and add to it over time. You might ask the young people to put some of their favorite music in the bin. The bin might include the following styles of music:

- *Prayerful, reflective instrumental music,* such as the kind that is available in the adult alternative section of music stores. Labels that specialize in this type of music include Windham Hill and Narada.
- *Popular songs with powerful messages.* If you are not well versed in popular music, ask the young people to offer suggestions.
- *The music of contemporary Catholic artists.* Many teens are familiar with the work of Catholic musicians such as Steve Angrisano, Sarah Hart, David W. Kauffman, Michael Mahler, Jesse Manibusan, and Danielle Rose.

Also consider including songbooks and hymnals. Many of the musical selections suggested in Total Youth Ministry are taken from the *Spirit & Song* hymnal, published by Oregon Catholic Press (OCP). If you wish to order copies of this hymnal, please contact OCP directly at *www.ocp.org* or by calling 800-548-8749. Including copies of your parish's chosen hymnal is a suitable option as well. You might also check with your liturgy or music director for recordings of parish hymns.

Some Closing Thoughts

We hope you find this material helpful as you invite young people into a deeper relationship with the marvelous community of faith we know as the Catholic Church. Please be assured of our continual prayers for you and the young people you serve.

Your Comments or Suggestions

Saint Mary's Press wants to know your reactions to the materials in the Total Youth Ministry series. We are open to all kinds of suggestions, including these:

- an alternative way to conduct an activity
- an audiovisual or other media resource that worked well with this material
- a book or an article you found helpful
- an original activity or process
- a prayer experience or service
- a helpful preparation for other leaders
- an observation about the themes or content of this material

If you have a comment or suggestion, please write to us at 702 Terrace Heights, Winona, MN 55987-1318; call us at our toll-free number, 800-533-8095; or e-mail us at *smp@smp.org.* Your ideas will help improve future editions of Total Youth Ministry.

Part A

Introductory Article

1 The Ministry of Youth Leadership Development

"True ministry duplicates itself."

This quote from the United States Catholic Conference's *Vision of Youth Ministry* (p. 10) continues to have relevance for ministry with young people. When adult leaders in youth ministry invest time and energy in the training and formation of young people, amazing results are produced. Young people become empowered to provide leadership for their peers in youth ministry groups, with adults in parish ministries, and among their friends and fellow students at school and in the community. They grow in confidence, have the skills necessary to participate fully in the life of the parish, and develop the abilities necessary to be a strong witness of faith. This investment in the young people of the parish has a long-term impact on the young people and on our Church and society.

As *Renewing the Vision* states: "We strongly encourage all ministry leaders and communities to call forth the gifts of all young people and empower them for ministry to their peers and leadership in our faith communities. We need their gifts, energy, and vitality" (United States Conference of Catholic Bishops, p. 42).

Who Is a Leader?

There was a time when leadership was seen as residing only in those who had "up-front" roles or were elected to official positions. Today a leader is anyone who uses their gifts, talents, skills, and abilities for the good of others. Some do this by serving on youth boards, parish councils, retreat teams, and peer ministry groups, and in other official roles. Many young people lead through volunteer service, sharing faith with their peers, and their everyday life choices.

Adolescents are in the process of discovering who they are. Each year they uncover gifts they possess that they didn't know they had. With time, they move from being "just beginners" to being accomplished masters of certain skills and abilities. Adults can help them name their gifts, provide

Reflect

"It was really amazing how God let me be my own kind of leader. There was this girl there who wrote a letter saying she was crying every night and she just wanted to go home and she didn't feel that she fit in and she gave this letter to me and so I would sit with her at lunch every day and I would talk to her and it was really amazing how God let me be a leader in my own way in just helping other people. I didn't necessarily have to be the chair of a committee or in charge of certain things." (A youth interviewed for "Effective Practices")

Reflect

Young leaders include those who do the following things:

◆ serve on a leadership body for the youth ministry program
◆ serve in liturgical ministries
◆ serve on parish committees
◆ volunteer in parish ministries
◆ volunteer with community service organizations
◆ display leadership qualities in their interactions with peers
◆ hold leadership positions within their school
◆ are leaders within a community organization

What Do You Think?

◆ How broad is the role of youth leadership in your thoughts about parish life?
◆ How are you open to the various ways that youth make a difference for the good of others?

practice and feedback while they try out new skills, offer support as they try new things, and walk with them through the successes and failures. We need to affirm and support young people in all the ways that they lead, and provide them with the training and opportunities necessary to grow into the types of leaders that God calls them to be.

The Whole Parish Has a Role to Play

When parishes intentionally prepare youth for their roles as leaders and provide training and formation for leadership, they reap the benefits of their efforts. Findings from "Effective Youth Ministry Practices in Catholic Parishes," a 2002 research project sponsored by the Center for Ministry Development and Saint Mary's Press, in collaboration with the National Federation for Catholic Youth Ministry, confirm the following points:

• Parish leadership programs help youth to grow in their own faith and to appreciate the growth of their peers' faith.
• Young people are doing surprising things in the parish. When given the opportunity to lead, they gain self-esteem, become active in the parish, and develop as religious leaders.
• Youth are willing, excited, passionate leaders in the parish. They share their gifts and energy as leaders in parish life and in ministry to their peers.

For the ministry of youth leadership development to succeed, the whole parish must participate. Youth ministry can ensure that young people are invited, trained, and supported, but every parish organization, ministry, event, and leadership structure within the parish should open itself to the gifts of young people. Young people can use their gifts and talents in liturgical ministries, as members of a choir, in service on the parish council, as members of the planning committee for the parish festival, or as members of the liturgy committee. Youth can work alongside adults on parish community service projects and social activities. And, of course, youth can lead their peers and younger children in youth ministry and catechetical programs. When the opportunities for leadership within the parish are that broad, every young person has the opportunity to use his or her unique gifts when and where they are best suited. Young people will feel a part of the parish community and will know that their gifts are valued beyond the youth ministry program. And the parish will be enlivened by the unique gifts of youth.

Helping Youth Develop as Leaders

We never want to expect young people to produce results without making sure they have the knowledge, training, and resources necessary to succeed. Youth are not miniadults; they are adolescents, with all the unfinishedness that accompanies that status. We should celebrate their energy and excitement, and treasure the growing faith that they are willing to share with their peers. But we must also be patient with the giggles, mistakes, embarrassed glances, and insecurity that can accompany young people through their initial attempts at leadership. We should praise the courage that it takes for youth to lead, while providing all the assistance necessary for them to do a good job of it.

No one, regardless of age, can master new skills immediately, which is why training, mentoring, and support are necessary as people work to become leaders. By using the ideas, strategies, and sessions in this manual, your parish can help its young people mature into strong Christian leaders. Remember, true ministry duplicates itself. Youth who are called, trained, and supported in leadership roles serve with great passion and energy. They develop amazing abilities to share faith, witness their relationship with God through the decisions they make, and pursue good works into adulthood.

People who are given the chance to lead when they are adolescents feel a stronger commitment to the Catholic Church as adults, and often base decisions about their life's work on positive initial experiences of faith and service that they had as adolescents. Adult leaders are in a unique position to make a lasting difference in the lives of youth—and the more opportunities we provide them to learn and practice good Christian leadership, the better off we all will be!

Conclusion

On the subject of discipleship, John Paul II said, "This is what is needed . . . a church which is not afraid to require much, after having given much; which does not fear asking from young people the effort of a noble and authentic adventure, such as that of the following of the Gospel" ("Thirty-second World Day of Prayer for Vocations"). If we are going to be the Church that John Paul II speaks of, we must welcome young people into leadership, allowing them the opportunity to serve, lead, and enter into the adventure of discipleship.

This resource manual is specifically devoted to the ministry of youth leadership development. Youth learn, in part, from the example of adults, so while you put energy into the development of youth leaders, it is essential that you also develop the skills and abilities of the adults who work with the youth.

For Further Reflection

Anyone who knows the stories of Jesus' life and ministry knows something about his leadership style. Starting at the very beginning of his public works, he called others to leadership. Within three years, he changed some obscure fisherman and brothers into people who would change the world. Jesus told them what to do when they were confused, shared wisdom and insight when they were clueless, prodded and

Reflect

"We have a thing in our church called a core group. It is like a leadership program for the kids and it's amazing to see, for me at least, what is the effect the kids can have." (A youth participant interviewed for "Effective Practices")

"You have to be open to allowing the mistakes or that they may not be able to do it as fast, or as quickly, or as well as we or another adult could do it. There is patience to allowing (youth) leadership to develop." (An adult participant interviewed for "Effective Practices")

"Leadership is shown by the kids themselves. That they weren't just waiting for someone to tell them what to do." (A parish staff participant interviewed for "Effective Practices")

What Do You Think?

◆ How does your parish invite young people to be leaders?
◆ What aspects of your parish's life could be more infused with young people?
◆ What gifts do young people bring to leadership roles in your parish?

Reflect

"What gives me hope is seeing young people graduating from college and choosing careers because of their faith. It is important to them. This one girl is spending two years in Chile in service. Someone is choosing to be a youth minister and pursuing that. That gives me hope because of what we have provided for them in their high school years, nurtured that so that they pursued that in college and then pursued that long term." (An adult leader interviewed for "Effective Practices")

What Do You Think?

How are you providing the necessary leadership training and formation for the adults in your parish?

Reflect

John 13:1–8,12–15

pushed when they were unwilling or stubborn, and encouraged them when their confidence was failing or they were disheartened. When they were ready and able, he assigned them tasks, watched over their early efforts, and, finally, commissioned them for leadership. If we follow Jesus' example, we too will be able to develop leadership in others, and they in turn will be able to live out their call to discipleship. (Adapted from Sidney Buzzell and Bill Perkins, *The Leadership Bible,* p. 1204)

Prayer

We bless you Lord for our calling
for nurturing in each of us a disciple's heart
a heart that rejoices in your coming
a heart sustained by your Spirit
a heart encouraged by fellow disciples.
May there grow in each of our hearts
the disciple's commitment to serve
the disciple's willingness to learn
and the disciple's joy in becoming
a medium of your grace.
(Donal Harrington and Julie Kavanagh, *Prayer for Parish Groups,* p. 37)

Part B

Strategies

2 Using This Manual to Develop Youth Leadership

Overview

Young people deserve the opportunity to help direct the youth ministry efforts of their parishes, to actively participate in parish life, to use their natural talents, and to develop leadership skills. For youth to do all that, youth ministry must make a concerted effort to provide opportunities for them to lead, help them develop leadership skills, and mentor them while they develop as leaders. The sessions and minisession in this manual may be used in a variety of ways to ensure that young people get some of the training they need in order to succeed in leadership positions. You can use the strategies listed in this part of the manual to create a plan that will work for your parish.

Training for Everyone

Include these sessions as part of an overall youth ministry program:
• "Leadership Is Making a Difference for Good" (chapter 6)
• "Jesus on Leadership" (chapter 7)
• "Unexpected Leaders of the Bible" (chapter 8)
• "Naming and Claiming Gifts in Self and Others" (chapter 9)
• "Communication Skills" (chapter 10)

Here are other uses for some of the sessions and minisessions:
• Use the "Attentive Listening Skills" minisession (chapter 15) at the beginning of a retreat, extended event, or program year to help the young people learn the importance of being good listeners.
• Use the "Group Decision-Making Skills" minisession (chapter 17) with a group of young people who will be asked to make decisions about programs, fund-raisers, or other events.

Sessions and Minisessions That Complement One Another

By combining sessions and minisessions, you can provide extended training on a number of leadership skills.

Communication

- "Communication Skills" (chapter 10) + "Attentive Listening Skills" (chapter 15) + "Reflective Listening Skills" (chapter 16) provides a good overview of the communication process and ways of listening.
- "Communication Skills" + "Large-Group Communication" (chapter 14) provides a good overview of the communication process and of ways of being an effective communicator in a group setting.
- "Attentive Listening Skills" + "Reflective Listening Skills" concentrates on the skills needed to be a good listener.

Group Facilitation

- "Leading Group Discussions" (chapter 11) + "Attentive Listening Skills" + "Reflective Listening Skills" provides solid training for small-group facilitators.
- "Leading Group Discussions" + "Effective Meeting Skills" (chapter 18) provides training for group leaders in meetings.

Negotiation

- "Negotiating Skills" (chapter 12) + "Group Decision-Making Skills" (chapter 17) helps the participants learn the skills necessary to achieve win-win decisions.

Planning

- "Planning Skills" (chapter 13) + "Group Decision-Making Skills" + "Effective Meeting Skills" helps the participants develop the skills for planning in a meeting.

A Yearlong Model for Youth Leadership Training

Consider this format for providing youth leadership training through a yearlong effort.

Fall: Foundational Sessions

- "Leadership Is Making a Difference for Good"
- "Jesus on Leadership"

Winter: Communication Skills

- "Communication Skills"
- "Attentive Listening Skills"
- "Reflective Listening Skills"

Spring: Group Skills
- "Leading Group Discussions"
- "Negotiating Skills"

Summer: Affirmation
- "Unexpected Leaders of the Bible"
- "Naming and Claiming Gifts in Self and Others"

A Weekend-Long Model for Youth Leadership Training

The outline that follows illustrates one option for using the activities in this manual to create a weekend-long retreat. Use other resources to add community-building activities and to research good retreat designs and formats. Helpful resources to complement your design include these:

- Hakowski, Maryann. *Vine and Branches: Resources for Youth Retreats,* vol. 1 (1992), vol. 2 (1992), and vol. 3 (1994). Winona, MN: Saint Mary's Press.
- Eckert, Ann Marie, *Resources for Community Life* (2004). Total Youth Ministry series. Winona, MN: Saint Mary's Press.
- Rydberg, Denny. *Building Community in Youth Groups.* Loveland, CO: Group Publishing, 1985.

Friday Evening
- Community-building activities: selections from other resources (30 minutes)
- Focusing activity (chapter 6): "Leadership Collage" (30 minutes)
- Group activity (chapter 6): "Using Our Gifts: Skits" (20 minutes)
- Reflection activity (chapter 6): "Becoming a Leader" (10 minutes)
- Short break
- Group activity (chapter 7): "News Report Role-Plays" (30 minutes)
- Presentation (chapter 7): "Jesus' Leadership Qualities" (20 minutes)
- Reflection (chapter 7): "Personal Leadership Reflection" (10 minutes)
- Short break
- Prayer (chapter 6): "Bearing the Light" (20 minutes)

Saturday
- Prayer (chapter 10): "Listening to God" (5 minutes)
- Focusing activity (chapter 10): "A Picture Says a Thousand Words" (15 minutes)
- Presentation (chapter 10): "Play Ball" (10 minutes)
- Object lesson (chapter 10): "Roadblock Role-Plays" (25 minutes)
- Presentation (chapter 16) "Practicing Reflective Listening" (10 minutes)
- Group activity (chapter 10): "Ten Commandments of Communication" (10 minutes)

- Short break
- Focusing activity (chapter 15): "Let's Get Talking" (30 minutes)
- Presentation (chapter 15): "An Overview of Attending Skills" (10 minutes)
- Focusing activity (chapter 11): "Learning from Others" (10 minutes)
- Brainstorming activity (chapter 11): "Tips for Successful Facilitation" (20 minutes)
- Object lesson (chapter 11): "Practicing Facilitation Skills" (30 minutes)
- Long break (lunch and recreation)
- Focusing activity (chapter 18): "Meeting Chaos" (10 minutes)
- Object lesson (chapter 18): "Meeting Skills" (25 minutes)
- Icebreaker or stretching activity (10 minutes)
- Focusing activity (chapter 13): "Planning a Vacation" (15 minutes)
- Small-group discussion (chapter 13): "Small-Group Discussion" (10 minutes)
- Presentation (chapter 13): "Principles of Planning" (10 minutes)
- Object lesson (chapter 13): "Practicing Planning Skills" (20 minutes)
- Long break (dinner)
- Group activity (chapter 17): "Winter Ball Parenting" (35 minutes)
- Presentation (chapter 17): "A Decision-Making Process" (10 minutes)
- Short break
- Presentation (chapter 12): "Does Win-Win Exist in the Real World?" (20 minutes)
- Presentation (chapter 12): "Win-Win Negotiation" (15 minutes)
- Object lesson (chapter 12): "Practicing Win-Win Negotiation" (20 minutes)
- Social activity: chosen from another resource (60 minutes)
- Evening prayer (chapter 8): "Are You Listening?" (10 minutes)

Sunday Morning
- Reflection (chapter 9): "Naming and Claiming My Gifts—Self-Reflection" (10 minutes)
- Group activity (chapter 9): "Naming the Gifts in Others" (25 minutes)
- Presentation (chapter 9): "Called, Gifted, and Sent" (10 minutes)
- Conclusion: a Eucharist preparation session, and a Mass celebrating the participants' learning (optional)

Creating Parish Leadership Positions for Youth

AT A GLANCE

◆ Preparing the Staff
◆ Working with Parish Organizations and Ministries
◆ Creating Leadership Roles
◆ Looking Beyond the Parish

Overview

Like the adults of the parish, the young people have various interests, passions, and styles of participation. Some youth will be drawn to liturgical ministries, some to service, some to helping in the religious education program. When we think about providing opportunities for leadership, we have to be broad and move beyond the opportunities that are offered within youth ministry programs. We should work toward including youth more fully in all the leadership structures of our parishes. To do that we must build support for youth, prepare adults to work with youth, and open the door for youth to participate in parish life as leaders. The following strategies help pave the way to greater youth leadership within the parish.

Preparing the Staff

The support and collaboration of parish leaders is essential for youth leadership to succeed. The following ideas help prepare the parish staff for their role:

- **Study** *Renewing the Vision: A Framework for Catholic Youth Ministry* (United States Conference of Catholic Bishops, 1997) and discuss the following questions:
  - How can we demonstrate our support of youth ministry to the entire parish?
  - What leadership groups in the parish would benefit by learning about Renewing the Vision?
  - How can we encourage the development of youth leaders in our areas of ministry?
- **Assess the parish's youth-friendly barometer.** Talk honestly about the ministries, organizations, and events in the parish that could be more youth-friendly. Discuss strategies for making changes within the leadership to effect positive change. Discuss who is best able to communicate

the necessary changes to those involved and act as a unified team in communicating those changes.

- **Plan to make positive changes.** Use strategies in this manual to invite youth into parish leadership, to help adults become more comfortable with youth, and to prepare youth for participating in adult committees. Work together as a staff to create additional programs and supports for successful youth leadership.

Working with Parish Organizations and Ministries

Many adults in the parish serve in a variety of leadership roles, as chairs and members of committees, commissions, events, and ministries. Those adults are essential in welcoming young people and engaging them in the work of parish life. To help all leaders become engaged in assisting youth, consider the following ideas:

- **Meet with parish organizations.** Invite the members of the organizations into a conversation about youth ministry and the ways they can involve young people in leadership. Use the following talking points:
  - Think about your own adolescent years. What challenges did you face as a young person?
  - What hopes do you have for the young people of the parish?
  - What do you believe youth need most?
  - What do you hope youth gain from involvement in the Church?
  - Where would you like to see youth more involved?
- **Share the goals of youth ministry** and the broad nature of the current understanding of youth ministry. Use handout 1, "Youth Ministry and Youth Leadership Development." Address these questions:
  - How might young people be part of this ministry?
  - What gifts would they bring?
  - How could the gifts of young people be used?
  - Who would be willing to welcome and mentor young people into the ministry?
- **Communicate with parish organizations.** Through letters, newsletters, bulletin inserts, e-mails, or personal phone calls, let the organizations know the what, who, and why of youth ministry. Offer your help in discovering opportunities for youth leadership within the organizations. Ask for the names of adults who are willing to welcome and mentor young people into the ministry.
- **Preparation and training.** The following ideas may be used in preparing adult groups who will be welcoming young people into their ministries:
  - Outline the leadership training and other support you will offer the young people.

○ Use chapter 20, "Knowing Youth," to help the adults prepare for youth involvement.

○ Distribute handout 36, "Working Side by Side with Youth" (chapter 20), to all the adults participating in parish ministries.

○ Ask organizations and ministries to complete handout 2, "Parish Ministry Information Sheet," for distribution to the young people who will participate in ministry.

Creating Leadership Roles

Encouraging participation in something new is easier when a specific job description is available. The more that young people know about the commitments involved, the better the chance that they will be able to fulfill those commitments. Help parish committees recognize that they can involve youth in leadership without selecting them for an official position. Youth can work side by side with adults to provide leadership for an event, or to perform one part of a larger job. When developing job descriptions, be careful that adults have appropriate expectations of young people. If a job description seems too large, is too involved, demands too much time, or does not expect the best of young people, go back to the committee with specific concerns and see if changes are possible.

Consider the following process for creating leadership roles within parish organizations and ministries:

• List the activities, events, and other leadership opportunities that occur throughout the year.

• For each leadership opportunity, list the leadership tasks needed. Use handout 3, "Leadership Tasks," to help organizations with that effort. For example, the Saint Vincent de Paul Society runs a Thanksgiving food basket project. Many leadership tasks make the event a success: communicating to the parish, making arrangements with social service organizations, collecting the food, arranging the baskets, and delivering the baskets.

• Choose which leadership roles are most appropriate for the young people. Be realistic about what roles would best be served by a partnership of youth and adults. Use handout 4, "Leadership Roles," and invite the organizations to complete the form with as much information as possible.

Use the leadership job descriptions to invite and encourage participation by young people within the organizations and ministries of the parish. Those descriptions will help the organizations and ministries be more organized. Encourage all ministry leaders to develop clear leadership job descriptions and to use them for inviting adults and youth into ministry.

Looking Beyond the Parish

When creating leadership opportunities for young people of the parish, consider contacting local community centers, community service organizations, and the local school systems to determine the resources that are available through those agencies. When inviting youth into leadership, include the community organizations in addition to parish ministries to create many opportunities for youth to use their gifts in the service of others.

Youth Ministry and Youth Leadership Development

Youth Ministry Has Three Goals

- **"Goal 1:** To empower young people to live as disciples of Jesus Christ in our world today" (*Renewing the Vision,* p. 9).
- **"Goal 2:** To draw young people to responsible participation in the life, mission, and work of the Catholic faith community" (p. 11).
- **"Goal 3:** To foster the total personal and spiritual growth of each young person" (p. 15).

Youth Ministry Needs the Whole Parish Community to Minister to All the Youth of the Parish

- "Youth Ministry is the response of the Christian community to the needs of young people, and the sharing of the unique gifts of youth with the larger community" (*A Vision of Youth Ministry,* p. 6).
- "The Church and world need the faith, gifts, energy, and fresh ideas of young people" (*Renewing the Vision,* p. 50).
- "The comprehensive approach is not a single program or recipe for ministry. Rather, it provides a way for integrating ministry with adolescents and their families into the total life and mission of the Church, recognizing that the whole community is responsible for this ministry" (p. 19).

Youth Ministry Sees Each Parish as Ready and Able to Respond to Youth

- "If parishes are to be worthy of the loyalty and active participation of youth, they will need to become 'youth-friendly' communities in which youth have a conspicuous presence in parish life" (*Renewing the Vision,* p. 13).
- "*Renewing the Vision* is a blueprint for the continued development of effective ministry with young and older adolescents. Its expanded vision and strategy challenges leaders and their faith communities to address these challenges and to invest in young people today" (p. 7).

Youth Ministry Includes the Leadership Development of Youth

- "The ministry of Leadership Development *calls forth, affirms,* and *empowers* the diverse gifts, talents, and abilities of . . . young people in our faith communities" (*Renewing the Vision,* p. 40).
- "We strongly encourage all ministry leaders and communities to call forth the gifts of all young people and empower them for ministry to their peers and leadership in our faith communities. We need their gifts, energy, and vitality" (p. 42).

(The quotations in paragraphs 1–3 and 5–10 are from *Renewing the Vision: A Framework for Catholic Youth Ministry* [Washington, DC: United States Catholic Conference of Catholic Bishops USCCB, 2002]. Copyright © 1997 by the USCCB. Used with permission.)

(The quotation in paragraph 4 is from *A Vision of Youth Ministry,* by the USCCB [Washington, DC: USCCB, 1986]. Copyright © 1986 by the USCCB. Used with permission.)

Parish Ministry Information Sheet

Parish ministry: _____

Contact person (name, phone number, and e-mail address): _____

_____

What are the goals and objectives of this ministry?

What is the leadership structure of this ministry?

When and where do you meet (dates, days, times, and places)?

What do you do at the meetings?

Other information:

Leadership Tasks

Program _____

Leadership Tasks	**Needed Leadership Positions**

Leadership Tasks

Name the different tasks needed for this program to succeed:

1. _____

2. _____

3. _____

4. _____

5. _____

6. _____

7. _____

8. _____

9. _____

10. _____

11. _____

12. _____

13. _____

14. _____

15. _____

16. _____

17. _____

18. _____

19. _____

20. _____

Needed Leadership Positions

Which tasks should be combined to create a leadership position? Connect tasks that belong together naturally, but do not make the jobs too large.

Position: _____
Leadership tasks: _____
(List the task numbers from column 1)

Position: _____
Leadership tasks: _____
(List the task numbers from column 1)

Position: _____
Leadership tasks: _____
(List the task numbers from column 1)

Position: _____
Leadership tasks: _____
(List the task numbers from column 1)

Position: _____
Leadership tasks: _____
(List the task numbers from column 1)

Position: _____
Leadership tasks: _____
(List the task numbers from column 1)

Position: _____
Leadership tasks: _____
(List the task numbers from column 1)

Position: _____
Leadership tasks: _____
(List the task numbers from column 1)

Position: _____
Leadership tasks: _____
(List the task numbers from column 1)

Position: _____
Leadership tasks: _____
(List the task numbers from column 1)

Leadership Roles

Program: _____

Leadership tasks to be performed (from handout 3, "Leadership Tasks"):

1. _____
2. _____
3. _____
4. _____

5. _____
6. _____
7. _____
8. _____

Abilities needed (skills, attitudes, understandings):

1. _____
2. _____
3. _____
4. _____

5. _____
6. _____
7. _____
8. _____

Length of commitment:

How many days, weeks, months will be needed?

_____

How many hours will the job take?

_____

Specific dates for meetings, event:

_____

Training and resources (specific training, written records, help provided):

_____

_____

Supporters and coworkers:

_____

Person in charge of overall event (or supervisor):

_____

Contact person for information and help:

_____

Benefits to the leader and the organization (Why is this leadership role important and good?):

_____

Inviting Youth into Leadership

AT A GLANCE

- ◆ Assessing Interest
- ◆ Sharing Opportunities
- ◆ Helping Youth Succeed
- ◆ Recognizing Christian Leadership in the World
- ◆ Forming Youth as Leaders
- ◆ Getting Out of the Way: Allowing Youth to Lead

Overview

Usually we give the most attention to leaders who have been selected or elected to an official position. But often young people are leaders because of the service they offer in their schools, community, or parish, or by the example they set for their peers. The following are strategies for assessing the gifts and interests of youth, creating avenues for youth to hear about available opportunities, helping youth think of ways they can make a difference in the world, and developing leadership skills and abilities in youth.

Assessing Interest

Let young people know, in a variety of ways, that you want to include them in parish ministry and leadership. This should begin when they are very young and continue throughout their adolescence. If young people experience the Church as being open to their gifts, ideas, and interests, they are more likely to stay involved and make the parish a priority. The following are some ideas for assessing interests:

- **Distribute youth interest finders.** Use handout 5, "Youth Interest Finder," with young people to assess their interest in parish ministries and community opportunities. You can adapt the handout to your specific situation by listing only the ministries and opportunities available in your parish and community. (The copy of this handout on the CD-ROM is easy to modify.) Give the interest finder to young people who are just beginning in youth ministry, about to participate in the sacrament of Confirmation, entering the parish as new members, or during other youth ministry events. The assessment of their interests will point out the ministries and opportunities that should be most inclusive of youth.

- **Use special events.** If your parish is having a special youth Mass (such as for a World Youth Weekend or for graduation), use that opportunity to find out which liturgical ministries young people have an interest in, or which youth have special talents (for example, liturgical dance, music, or decorating) that could be called on. If young people help with a parish-wide event (for instance, a carnival, a liturgy, or a service project) as a part of the youth ministry program, invite them to serve on the committee for that event the following year.

- **Talk with youth.** Use everyday encounters and events to talk about leadership, ministry, and service roles available at the parish and in the community. Whenever possible, ask young people (in a group or individually) whether they are interested in those ministries.
- **Recognize leadership roles in other settings.** Many young people assume leadership roles in their schools and communities. Find out what your youth are involved in, support their efforts there, and use their talents, when possible, for parish ministry.

Sharing Opportunities

Take the time to let the young people know how they can be involved. Share with them the opportunities available in the parish and in the community. Have a "big event" once a year or introduce the young people to ministries one at a time. Whatever you choose, remember that you have to share information all the time. The following are some strategies for getting the word out:

- **Book guest speakers.** Invite leaders from parish ministries or community organizations to attend youth ministry events to talk about what their groups do and how young people can be involved. Those talks can be shared during the first 5 minutes at the start of a program or over dessert at a meal, as a quick way of letting the young people know about opportunities and helping them connect with adults of the parish and community.
- **Hold a ministry fair for youth.** Create a time when the leaders of parish ministries and community organizations can talk with youth about the ways they can be involved in their groups. Hold this event some afternoon, connect it with a larger youth gathering, or implement it after a Sunday liturgy.
- **Communicate through newsletters and Web pages.** Include information about opportunities for youth available throughout the parish. Highlight a different ministry each month, or supply a list of regularly occurring parish meetings where young people are encouraged to participate.

Helping Youth Succeed

By being attentive to young people who are joining mostly adult groups, you can help clear the path for those who will follow. Here are some strategies for success:

- **Talk about expectations.** Help the young people talk about what they hope will happen and what they are worried about. Help them name their own feelings about doing something new, and help them think through ways they can interact that will have a positive effect on the other members (adults) of the group.

- **Assign mentors.** Assign young people mentors from the ministries they join. Mentors help train young people, offering encouragement through any difficulties, sharing passion for the ministry, and providing support. To ensure the safety of the youth, assign either two adults to each young person or two youth to each adult.
- **Be available to address problems.** Let the parish ministry leaders and volunteers know you are available to help them if they have concerns or questions about a young person's participation in their ministry. Check in with parish leaders a few months after a young person has started participating, to make sure things are going smoothly.

Recognizing Christian Leadership in the World

By taking the time to talk with young people about the different ways members of their community live their faith on a daily basis, you can encourage young people to consider ways they can lead and live their own faith. Consider the following ideas:

- **Hold a panel discussion.** Invite five members of the community who are models of Christian leadership to participate in a panel discussion. Consider professionals (doctors, lawyers, teachers, and others) who make choices based on faith, people who volunteer their time to community organizations, parents who raise faith-filled children, and others. Invite the panelists to talk about why they have made the choices that they have and how they believe they are leaders (making a difference for good) within their lives.
- **Highlight Catholic leaders.** Highlight youth and adult members of the parish community in a parish newsletter or Web site. Write brief biographies of their lives and the choices they make that have a positive impact on others.

Forming Youth as Leaders

Young people, like all of us, need to practice new skills in order to master them. During leadership training, young people need the opportunity to try out the skills in "real life," and some further direction and support if they are going to master a new skill. By providing mentors and peer leadership groups, you give youth the opportunity to develop within a safe community that is dedicated to trying new skills, to developing leadership abilities, and to providing support for those who are new at leadership. Consider the following helps:

- **Assign mentors.** Mentors can share the journey with young people. Whether other youths or adults, mentors walk with the young people as they develop new skills and grow in faith. This is helpful when young people are involved in a specific ministry, such as being a lector, where they need someone who provides the specifics of the ministry, who is available to help them practice, and who can share their personal passion for the ministry.

- **Train and form a peer leadership team.** Consider adding an intentional training and formation layer to the current youth ministry leadership team. Be clear from the start that the team will receive training and will be expected to practice their leadership skills within the context of the leadership they provide for the parish youth ministry. Build in opportunities for feedback (both positive and constructive), support, and additional training throughout the year. The best way for youth to learn leadership skills is to have to use them over and over again.

- **Provide leadership training for everyone.** Many young people have leadership potential, but no one ever gives them the insight or the skills necessary to feel confident in the role of leader. Use the ideas in chapter 2, "Using This Manual to Develop Youth Leadership," to implement leadership training that becomes part of the ongoing youth ministry offerings.

Getting Out of the Way: Allowing Youth to Lead

When youth are not allowed in leadership roles, even though they have the skills and the abilities, they lose their desire to be involved or they get discouraged. One positive thing adults can do is to get out of the way. Consider these suggestions:

- **Know what young people can do.** Assess the abilities of the youth involved and know what they can and cannot do. When a young person has demonstrated the ability to lead prayer or an icebreaker, serve in a liturgical ministry, or run a service project, let him or her!

- **Watch for growth.** Keep your eyes open for emerging abilities and confidence. As young people mature, they are more and more capable of doing great things. Look for signs of that growth.

- **Let them fail.** One of the best ways to learn is by experiencing failure. You will have to make good decisions about when to allow young people to fail, but in some situations it is better for an individual or a group not to succeed than for you to jump in and save them. After allowing a failure, make sure you talk about the situation; help the young person or group understand what should have been done differently, and provide support and encouragement for them to continue to develop leadership.

- **Provide ongoing direction and support.** By letting young people lead, you give them confidence, and by providing them with support and direction, you help them continue to develop and grow. It is important not to stifle leadership attempts, but you need to be attentive to how much direction a new leader needs to achieve success. It is hard to always get it right, but try to provide only enough direction and support for success.

- **Do not be afraid to critique.** By being clear about what young people are doing well and what they need to continue to work on, you help them to develop skills, grow as individuals, and master their own emotions and reactions. This is important work for adolescence, and you can play an important role in their lives if you are willing to speak the truth.

Youth Interest Finder

Name: _____

Address: _____

Phone number: _____ E-mail address: _____

Leadership Opportunities in Youth Ministry

Community or Society

❑ Welcome others into the community.

❑ Minister to peers by listening to them and referring them to resources.

❑ Plan and organize youth ministry events and projects.

❑ Plan and organize fund-raising projects.

❑ Help plan and conduct social events such as dances, lock-ins, and movie nights.

❑ Help plan and conduct sports events such as volleyball, basketball, and baseball games.

❑ Help plan and conduct outdoor events such as skiing, canoeing, and camping experiences.

❑ Help plan and conduct trips.

Service

❑ Plan and conduct service projects.

❑ Organize and implement fund-raisers for people and projects in need.

Spirituality

❑ Help lead and present retreats for youth.

❑ Help prepare other youth for the sacrament of Confirmation.

❑ Help plan prayer opportunities for youth.

Worship

❑ Help plan and implement special youth liturgies.

❑ Help plan and implement a youth Reconciliation service.

❑ Serve on the parish worship committee.

❑ Share musical talents: (List specific musical talents.)

Communication

❑ Write articles for the youth newsletter.

❑ Help edit and produce the youth newsletter.

❑ Help with artwork for the youth newsletter and flyers.

❑ Help with photography at events.

❑ Write news releases for local papers.

❏ Help design flyers and do publicity.

❏ Help get the word out at your school.

List other skills, gifts, and interests that you could offer to the community:

_____

_____

_____

Leadership Opportunities in the Parish Community

Community

❏ Welcome others into the community.

❏ Plan and organize junior high ministry events and projects.

❏ Participate in and share leadership in parish fund-raising projects.

❏ Help plan and share leadership in parish community-building events, such as a picnic or a festival.

Service and Outreach

❏ Assist in service projects of the parish outreach team.

❏ Assist in fund-raising projects of the parish mission team.

Spirituality

❏ Help plan and staff junior high retreats.

❏ Help prepare children for sacraments.

❏ Help plan and prepare for parish spirituality projects, such as the parish mission and Lenten and Advent programs.

Worship and Liturgy

❏ Help prepare and implement a children's liturgy of the word.

❏ Serve as a liturgy commission representative.

❏ Serve as a Eucharistic minister.

❏ Serve as a lector.

❏ Serve as a minister of hospitality.

❏ Assist with art and environment needs.

❏ Participate in the choir.

❏ Serve as a cantor.

❏ Serve as a Eucharistic minister to people who are homebound.

❏ Help write the prayers of the faithful for Mass.

❏ Write a brief article for the bulletin, reflecting on Sunday Scripture readings.

❏ Play musical instruments for parish functions: (List the instruments.)

Religious Education

- ❏ Serve as a teacher.
- ❏ Serve as a teacher's aide.
- ❏ Serve as a coteacher for junior high or high school faith formation.
- ❏ Serve as a religious education or youth ministry board member.
- ❏ Help in the office with administrative tasks.
- ❏ Assist with nursery or preschool programs.

Communication

- ❏ Help with photography at parish events.
- ❏ Write articles for the church bulletin.
- ❏ Write news releases for local papers.
- ❏ Help design flyers and do publicity for parish events.
- ❏ Assist with the development or ongoing support of a parish Web site.

5 Strategies for Parents of Young Leaders

Overview

As young people develop their skills and take advantage of new leadership opportunities, they need support from home if they are to succeed. Parents who support, help solve problems, talk with, and mentor young people in leadership roles are ensuring that those children have a positive leadership experience. The following strategies help parishes provide parents with information and specific ideas for helping their children blossom as Christian leaders.

Methods of Reaching Parents

If leadership is *making a difference for good,* then there are myriad ways for young people to lead. Sharing that good news with parents accomplishes two goals: it lets them know you have recognized the leadership qualities in their children, and it tells them that leadership comes in many forms. Most parents can use some help from their parishes in thinking through ways to help their children learn, grow, and develop as Christian leaders. Consider these ideas:

- **Write to parents.** Congratulate parents on the qualities their young people possess. Make the letter specific so that parents can know the gifts and talents you have recognized in their sons and daughters.
- **Speak with parents one-on-one.** If a young person is serving in an official ministry, speak with the parents so that they can know firsthand the valuable service their daughter or son is providing. When you see parents (when teenagers are dropped off or picked up, at Sunday liturgy, at the supermarket, and so on), share some good news with them.
- **Create a leader bulletin board or Web site.** Use a bulletin board or Web site to highlight the good works that young people do. Include young people who serve in up-front leadership roles and those who lead from within organizations and among their peers. Send parents a postcard or a letter letting them know that their son or daughter will be highlighted.

- **Gather parents together.** Plan for refreshments and other elements that make for a good meeting. Provide time for parents to get to know one another and for you to let them know how their sons and daughters are involved in leadership.
- **Parishwide communication.** Insert handout 6, "Supporting Your Child as a Leader," into the parish bulletin, post it on the parish Web site, or publish it in the parish newsletter.

Elements of a Parents' Meeting

Include these elements in a meeting for parents of youth leaders, or use them separately when appropriate.

Discernment

Young people often overextend themselves. Though their intentions are good, their follow-through can be frustrating to all involved. Here are some ideas for helping youth and parents discern opportunities:

- Invite parents and youth to rank the following roles in terms of their priority in the life of the young people: family, school, youth ministry leadership after-school activities, job, community activities, sports, band, and others. You may wish to have the parents and the youth gather in peer groups, or have each family group complete the ranking. Walking parents and youth through this process will help them determine whether the young people have the time and energy to make parish leadership opportunities a priority. If they are more committed to other things, this process will help them acknowledge that.
- Ask parents to list all the activities their children are active in. Include family obligations, school commitments, parish roles and activities, jobs, and so forth. Ask the parents to rank the activities by how important they (the parents) believe they are in the lives of their children. Encourage the parents to invite their children to do the same, and then talk about the similarities and differences (if any) in the rankings. Encourage parents to recognize that their young people cannot succeed in everything and that they often need help setting priorities.

Leadership Opportunities

Talk about the roles young people play in the parish and the opportunities that are available to them within the community. Here are some ways to do that:

- Invite a group of young people to create a skit of the leadership roles they play in the parish.
- Create a video showing the variety of ways youth are involved in leadership and show it to parents.
- Create a list of youth leadership roles and the specific duties of those roles. If possible, include the length of each commitment, the training

provided, outside-the-meeting work that needs to be done, and so forth. Present the report in an electronic format.

- Invite a young person to talk about why he or she values the leadership role or roles he or she has assumed—including what he or she has learned, how he or she is serving, and why it is important to be involved.

Leadership Training

Describe the leadership training provided for youth leaders, including the expectations you have for participation in the training, the cost, the length of time, and other details. Here are two ideas for helping parents recognize and support the importance of training:

- Invite a young person to talk about a leadership camp experience, a training program, or a mentoring relationship.
- Provide an overview of the skills the young people will learn. Teach a skill to the parents to highlight the level of training that will be provided.

Sharing

Giving parents the opportunity to talk with other parents about the struggles and joys of raising young leaders is helpful. Offer these opportunities for sharing:

- Ask the parent of an active youth leader to give a talk about the value of their child's leadership opportunity and the way the family supports such leadership roles.
- Invite parents to share with other parents how they manage the struggles associated with having leadership youth in the house—coping with overextended schedules, organizing car pooling, balancing family life, and seeking rest and relaxation.
- Invite a couple of youth leaders to talk about the ways their families support them. Invite the parents to ask questions or to talk with the young people about what is helpful and not helpful.
- Invite parents to talk about the ways they served as leaders when they were young. Have them share about the struggles, joys, and frustrations of leadership during their own adolescence.

Parents' Expertise

Encourage parents to help you involve young people more fully in the parish and community. Consider using methods such as these:

- Invite parents to brainstorm ways the gifts and talents of young people could be used within the parish or a community organization that they themselves are involved in.
- Ask parents to name the gifts and talents of their children and of other teenagers they know.
- Ask for help providing training to young people. Many parents have leadership training and expertise from their workplace or volunteer activities. Invite parents to help train youth in specific leadership skills.

- Let parents know you are available to talk with them about their sons and daughters' leadership involvement. Keep the lines of communication open!

Prayer

Include handout 7, "The Lord's Prayer for Parents," during the meeting, or as a prayer resource. If you use the prayer at the meeting, have a leader read the lines from the official Lord's Prayer (in roman print) and invite the parents to read the reworded lines (in italicized print).

Supporting Your Child as a Leader

Parents of Christian Leaders . . .

Model Leadership

Consider these three rules for raising children:

- Be a good role model.
- Be a good role model.
- Be a good role model.

Parents who assume leadership positions themselves raise young people who view leading and serving as a natural part of life and find it easier to step into those roles. Ask yourself: In what ways do I model Christian leadership in my home, parish, and community?

Are Informed

Read newsletters and bulletins; check Web sites; converse with teachers, youth ministers, and the other adults in your child's life; and attend meetings. Learn as much as you can about the leadership roles your child has taken on, the ministry that is being performed, or the possibilities for leadership that are available. Ask yourself: How much do I know about what my child is doing in his or her role as leader?

Set Goals and Priorities

Overextended lifestyles make it easy to spend time on activities that do not produce long-range benefits to the quality of life. Family discussions about values clarification, goals, and priorities help your child (and you) make better choices about time management. Ask yourself: How do I help my child set goals and priorities?

Show Support by Sharing Resources

Support organizations, agencies, and activities that reflect your family values and offer leadership opportunities for your child. Volunteer to drive, chaperone, provide treats, or make phone calls. Share your suggestions for improvements and offer to help. Thank the adults in charge. Your small investment can produce big results by helping those programs to thrive. Ask yourself: What gifts do I have to share?

Encourage Participation

Mark your calendar and put flyers on the refrigerator. Talk to your son or daughter, his or her friends, and the friends' parents. Most young people need encouragement and reminders—so do not be shy about putting in a good word for programs you consider worthwhile. Ask yourself: Do I have any creative ways to encourage participation?

Acknowledge Accomplishments

Recognizing accomplishments that uphold values and a willingness to serve without rewards is important when nurturing Christian leadership skills. When your child demonstrates those skills, tell her or him that you're proud, again and again, through scrapbooks, refrigerator displays, a family Web site, and so on. Ask yourself: How does our family celebrate accomplishments and positive behavior?

Communicate

Eating together, riding in a car, and sharing hobbies and chores are all ways to generate conversation. The more you listen to your child, the more likely you are to discover unique gifts, talents, and leadership skills. Ask yourself: In what special way does our family communicate?

Pray

Pray for and with your son or daughter. Mealtime prayers, family rosary times, or going to church as a family all help keep the focus on using gifts and talents in a Christlike way. Ask yourself: What time does our family set aside for prayer?

Help Solve Problems

Invite your child to talk with you when she or he is having difficulty, and listen carefully to the concerns. While young people are developing as leaders, they may not always know the best way to handle a crisis or a difficult person. Provide guidance as they try out new skills, learn new ways of dealing with their emotions, and succeed in their leadership roles. Ask yourself: What leadership skills do I have that I could share with my child?

The Lord's Prayer for Parents

Our Father who art in heaven,

Our loving God, as the Father of us all, you understand our concerns as parents.

hallowed be thy name.

From your view, Lord, our lives take on an entirely different perspective. We call on you, with respect and confidence, to hear our prayer.

Thy kingdom come.

Thy will be done on earth, as it is in heaven.

Help us to be a part of your divine plan in all that we do. Help our families to be a part of your everlasting Kingdom.

Give us this day our daily bread,

Help us to provide for all the spiritual and temporal needs of our children.

and forgive us our trespasses,

Forgive us for the times when we have hurt our spouses or our children,

as we forgive those who trespass against us,

as we strive to love our families unconditionally, as you love us.

and lead us not into temptation,

but deliver us from evil.

And protect us all from the evils of this world and help us live together in holiness with you forever.

Amen.

(The words of the Lord's Prayer on this handout are quoted from the English translation of the *Catechism of the Catholic Church* for use in the United States of America, no. 2759. Copyright © 1994 by the United States Catholic Conference, Inc.—Libreria Editrice Vaticana.)

(The words in italics are from Kathleen Kensinger, Ralston, Nebraska, and are used with permission.)

Part C

Leadership Sessions

6 Leadership Is Making a Difference for Good

AT A GLANCE

Study It

Core Session:
A Light in the Darkness
(60 minutes)

◆ Leadership Collage
(30 minutes)

◆ Using Our Gifts: Skits
(20 minutes)

◆ Becoming a Leader
(10 minutes)

Pray It

◆ Bearing the Light
(20 minutes)

Overview

This session helps the young people discover that leadership means much more than just being the up-front person—that it means making a difference for good in the world. The session explains that young people are called to leadership regardless of the positions they hold or the personality traits they possess. It points out that leaders are servants of those they lead—and that they carry out their role with the help of the Holy Spirit.

Outcomes

◆ The participants will reflect on the traits and characteristics of a Christian leader.

◆ The participants will explore the importance of the gifts for leadership that they and others have been given.

◆ The participants will be introduced to a unique leadership process and its four key elements.

Background Reading

◆ Scriptural connections: John 1:1–9 (The Word became flesh), John 13:1–17 (Jesus washes the disciples' feet), 1 Cor. 12:12–22 (The Church is one body with many members)

◆ *Catholic Youth Bible* article connections: "Leaders with Character" (Prov. 6:16–19), "Prayer of a Servant Leader" (Luke 22:24–27), "True Greatness" (Matt. 20:20–28), "Christian Leadership" (Titus 1:5–9)

Study it!

Familyconnections

◆ Invite the families to look through a week's worth of newspapers and cut out articles and pictures that represent concerns of the world. Suggest that they place those articles and pictures where everyone in the family can see them daily, and pray for those concerns at family dinners.

◆ Encourage the families to talk about the ways each family member makes a difference in the world. Ask them to spend one family meal or car ride talking about something good they have done for someone else during the past week.

Core Session:
A Light in the Darkness (60 minutes)

Preparation

- Gather the following items:
  - ❑ issues of current news magazines and sections of current newspapers, at least one for each participant
  - ❑ glue sticks, one for every three or four participants
  - ❑ scissors, one for every three or four participants
  - ❑ poster board, one piece for every three or four participants
  - ❑ masking tape
  - ❑ *Catholic Youth Bibles* or other Bibles, one for every six to eight participants
  - ❑ copies of handout 8, "Becoming a STARRR," one for each participant
  - ❑ pens or pencils
  - ❑ a tape player or a CD player
  - ❑ tapes and CDs of reflective instrumental music
- Set up a space, preferably on tables, where the participants can work in groups of three or four. Consider covering the work surfaces because the participants will be using glue sticks. At each location place a variety of magazines and newspaper sections, glue sticks, scissors, and a piece of poster board.

Leadership Collage (30 minutes)

1. Gather the participants into a large group. Welcome them and then offer these thoughts:

- Many things (including hate, war, prejudice, and violence) cloud the world in darkness. Christian leaders are beacons of light that can lead us out of the darkness. They are lights that overcome the shadows and evils in the world.

- Bright lights such as Martin Luther King Jr. and Mother Teresa inspire us and serve as role models of true Christian leadership. However, name recognition is not a prerequisite for making a difference for good.

- Anyone can be a leader. The student who spends Saturday mornings working at a camp for children with disabilities, and encourages others to come along too, is a Christian leader. The parent who faithfully supports and cares for a family, while making time to serve on church and community committees, is another. The teacher who takes a personal interest in discovering the unique gifts of every student also models Christian leadership.

2. Ask the participants these two questions. Invite them to respond verbally or offer them time for quiet reflection.
• Who are the models of leadership in your life?
• Who does the world look to for light in the darkest days?

3. Assign the participants to small groups of three or four. Invite the groups to gather around the prepared work surfaces. Then give these instructions:
• From the magazines and newspapers provided, cut out pictures of people you consider to be good Christian role models. You can also choose words or images that remind you of Christian leaders.
• As a group, arrange and glue the pictures, words, and images into a collage on the poster board.
• You will have 10 minutes to complete this task.

4. Display the groups' finished collages where all can view them. As you do so, invite the participants to look at the work of the other small groups. Then engage the participants in a discussion using the following questions:
• Which picture, word, or image says the most to you about Christian leadership?
• What distinguishes a Christian leader from any other type of leader? [Possible responses are "Christian leaders operate from a set of values based on Jesus' values" and "Christian leaders have a relationship with Jesus."]

5. Present the following information to the participants:
• Personality traits are different from character traits. Personality traits (for instance, a sense of humor and an outgoing attitude) set people apart; character traits are deeper qualities, such as moral strength and self-discipline.
• Personality refers to how people act or present themselves. Character refers to who people really are.
• Though leaders seem to share certain traits, those shared traits are not the only things that make a leader, because not all circumstances require the same set of leadership skills. For example, a good coach does not necessarily make a good pastor.

6. Ask the participants for more examples of leaders who might not perform well in a different situation. Urge them to explain why one leadership style might not work in another leadership setting. Then continue your presentation with the following comments:

Mediaconnections

◆ *Lucas* (Twentieth Century Fox, 100 minutes, 1986, rated PG-13). This movie depicts a young man who leads his football team but not on the field.

◆ *Pay It Forward* (Warner Brothers, 123 minutes, 2000, rated PG-13). This movie demonstrates the idea that making a difference for good can change the world.

◆ *Remember the Titans* (Disney Studios, 114 minutes, 2002, rated PG). This movie portrays a man who has a profound impact on a community through the leadership he provides to his football team and the community.

- Not all leaders use their gifts to make a difference for good. Some leaders seek power, money, fame, or recognition. Adolph Hitler, for example, was a strong leader, but he definitely was not a leader for good.
- What current leaders make a difference for good?

Using Our Gifts: Skits (20 minutes)

1. Introduce this activity by making the following comments:

- Through Jesus' example, we know that helping others—making a difference for good—is something we should all do. The Christian faith tells us we are all called to be leaders, people who make a difference for good.
- The primary difference between Christian leaders and secular leaders is that all Christian leaders are followers of Christ and not all secular leaders are.
- Baptized members of the Church are called to use their gifts and talents, whatever those may be, in service to the world.

2. Form small groups of six to eight people. Give each group a Bible, and invite the groups to read 1 Cor. 12:12–22 and then discuss what that passage says about making a difference for good. Give the groups 5 minutes for discussion.

3. Invite each group to devise a skit, a role-play, or a pantomime to present the Scripture passage and what it says to them about leadership and making a difference for good. Allow the groups 10 minutes to develop and rehearse their ideas. While the groups are rehearsing, create a stage area for the presentations. Have a few chairs available in case the groups need them for quick set changes.

4. Invite the groups to gather in the stage area. Invite one of the groups to present its skit, followed by the other groups. Ask each group to begin by setting the stage (such as by describing the location of the skit or introducing their roles) for the audience.

5. When all the presentations have concluded, ask the following questions:

- What do all these presentations tell us about our own gifts?
- What do the presentations tell us about others' gifts?
- As leaders, what are we called to do?

6. Read John 13:2–6, beginning at the last sentence of verse 2: "And during supper . . ." Allow a moment for quiet reflection, then offer the following comments:

- Jesus requires us to serve each other, and in so doing, to serve him.

- It does not matter whether we are an arm or a leg, a hand or an ear. It does not matter whether we are young or old, rich or poor. Whatever our gifts, we are called to share them with the world. This is the idea of Christian leadership.

Becoming a Leader (10 minutes)

1. Distribute handout 8 and pens or pencils. Offer some comments about the four elements listed on the handout:

- *See a need in your world.* Leadership is all about making a difference, but we must have our eyes and hearts open if we are going to recognize where we can help.
- *Tell God about it in prayer.* We cannot change the whole world, but we can pray for anyone and anything. Our prayer often helps us recognize how we can use our gifts to make a difference.
- *Assess your unique gifts and talents.* Figuring out what gifts you have to offer is an important part of the process. Everyone makes a difference in their own way, using the gifts they have. Doing things your way is important.
- *Respond. Take the **R**isk. **R**each out.* Too often, even when we see a need, we do not act. Leadership means responding!

2. Invite the participants to take 5 minutes to complete the handout. You might play reflective music during this time.

3. Invite the participants to take the handout with them and to put it somewhere noticeable—on their bedroom mirror, inside their locker, or another place that will remind them of how they can be a STARRR. Conclude by making the following points:

- If you really want to follow Jesus' example, you will use the gifts and talents God has given you—even the things you don't always think about as gifts.
- If you have perseverance, you can find something you really believe in and dedicate your time to it. If you are quiet and reflective, you might speak the truth through poetry, writing, or storytelling. Each of us leads differently, depending on the situation and on our particular set of gifts.
- Ultimately, we are called to lead others through our words, actions, decisions, and faith. Sometimes we do that as up-front leaders, but most of the time we lead from within.

TryThis

In later gatherings remind the participants to continue to act as leaders and to make a difference for good. You might invite them to share what they have done to become a STARRR in the past week or month.

Spirit & Song connections

- ◆ "Christ, Be Our Light," by Bernadette Farrell
- ◆ "Christ Will Be Your Light," by David Haas
- ◆ "Go Light Your World," by Chris Rice

TryThis

Keep the articles, pictures, and stars and display them in the back of the church or in a gathering space in the parish, to remind the young people of the world's needs and their gifts.

Bearing the Light (20 minutes)

Preparation

- Gather the following items:
  - ❏ sections of newspapers from the past week, at least one for each participant
  - ❏ scissors, one for every two to four participants
  - ❏ glue sticks, one for every three or four participants
  - ❏ sheets of black construction paper, one for each participant
  - ❏ 5-inch stars cut out of bright-colored paper, three or four for each participant
  - ❏ markers
  - ❏ a *Catholic Youth Bible* or other Bible, marked at John 1:1–9
  - ❏ a candle and matches or a lighter
  - ❏ a cloth
  - ❏ newsprint
  - ❏ masking tape
  - ❏ copies of *Spirit & Song* or another hymnal, one for each participant
- Set up a worktable for every three or four students, with the newspaper sections, scissors, glue sticks, sheets of black construction paper, stars, and markers on each table.
- Place the Bible and the candle on the cloth on the floor to designate a prayer space. The participants should have enough room to sit on the floor in a circle around the cloth.
- On newsprint write these two prayer statements and responses:
  Statement 1: Lord, we seek you in the shadow of . . .
  Response 1: Lord, show us your light.
  Statement 2: Lord, I offer you my gift of . . .
  Response 2: Lord, help us bear your light.
- Invite a participant to proclaim the Scripture reading.
- Select a closing song from the *Spirit & Song* Connections in this chapter or from another hymnal.

    1. Organize the participants into small groups of three or four. Direct the groups to the tables you have set with the necessary supplies. Then give the following instructions:

- Look through a section of a newspaper. Find an article or picture about a problem that you are concerned about, cut it out, and glue it to a piece of black construction paper. You have 2 minutes to complete this activity.

When time is up, give the next instruction:

- Take three or four stars and a marker from the table. Think about the other people in your group and the gifts that each possesses. When you have thought of a gift for each person, write it on a star for that person.
- Think about your own gifts, and write one of them on a star for yourself.

After 2 minutes, encourage the participants to share their stars with the other members of their small groups. Explain that they should not just give the stars to one another, but tell one another why they wrote what they did. Give the groups no more than 5 minutes for this sharing.

2. Invite the participants to bring their stars and their news articles or pictures to the prayer circle. Ask them to sit on the floor around the Bible and the candle. Distribute the hymnals you have chosen. Explain the prayer as follows:

- Today's prayer focuses on being light in the darkness. Each of you holds in your hands both light and darkness. We want to bring the needs of the world to prayer today.
- You will be asked to name the need, or darkness, that you saw in the article or picture you chose. When it is time, I will invite each of you, in turn, to say, "Lord, we seek you in the shadow of . . ." and name the darkness. We will all respond, "Lord, show us your light." [Refer the participants to the phrases you have noted on newsprint.]
- You will also be asked to name the gift that you have recognized in yourself and that others have seen in you. When it is time, I will invite you each, in turn, to say, "Lord, I offer you my gifts of . . ." We will all respond, "Lord, help us bear your light." [Again refer them to the phrases you have noted on newsprint.]

Ask a participant to light the candle, and begin the prayer with the sign of the cross.

Invite the volunteer to proclaim John 1:1–9. Allow a moment for quiet reflection. Then say the following prayer:

> Lord, we come together to ask for the light of your presence in the dark areas of the world. We ask for you to help each of us become a bearer of your light. As we name these needs today, Lord, we place them in your circle of light.

Call the participants to begin their sharing. Note that when it is their turn, they should stand, place their news picture or article on the floor near the candle, and proclaim statement 1. Then everyone else should recite response 1.

3. After everyone has shared once, lead the prayer around the circle again, this time with the participants taking turns laying their stars on the newspaper articles where they might do the most good, while proclaiming statement 2. After each person prays, lead everyone in offering response 2.

4. Invite the participants to join in singing the closing song you have selected.

Becoming a STARRR

See a need in your world. To be leaders we have to keep our eyes open to the needs around us—within our families, communities, schools, parishes, countries, and world. It takes practice to open our eyes and hearts to see the needs, great and small, that surround us every day.
What is a need you see?

Tell God about the need in prayer. Everything starts with prayer. Coming before God with specific needs and asking for his presence in those areas opens the door to the work of the Holy Spirit.
Take a moment for prayer.

Assess your unique gifts and talents and decide what you have to bring to the need you see. God has gifted you in the special ways that make you the person you are. Acknowledging those gifts shows appreciation for them and helps you to humbly realize that your life is an important part of God's plan.
How can you use your gifts to make a difference?

Respond. Take the **R**isk. **R**each out. It takes courage to lead, but you've already asked for God's help, so you have reason to feel confident. Go ahead and offer what you have to give. It's time to let your light shine!
What will you do immediately to respond? What might take more time?

Study It

Core Session:
Jesus on Leadership
(60 minutes)

- ◆ News Report Role-Plays
  (30 minutes)
- ◆ Jesus' Leadership Qualities
  (20 minutes)
- ◆ Personal Leadership
  Reflection
  (10 minutes)

Pray It

- ◆ Hearing the Call to Lead
  (10 minutes)

Live It

- ◆ Want ads
- ◆ Thank-you notes

7 Jesus on Leadership

Overview

As Christians we are called to follow the example of Jesus in the ways that we live. That call includes the way we use our gifts and talents in leadership roles. This session invites the participants to reflect on the ways Jesus led— providing insight into the leadership qualities that Christian leaders should strive for.

Outcomes

- ◆ The participants will explore and use Scripture stories to uncover characteristics of Jesus' leadership style.
- ◆ The participants will compare qualities of Jesus' leadership style with those of their own leadership styles.

Background Reading

- ◆ "Qualities of Effective Leaders," found on the CD-ROM
- ◆ *Catholic Youth Bible* article connections: "We Are the Body of Christ" (Rom. 12:1–8), "Divine Humility, Cosmic Glory" (Phil. 2:1–11)

Core Session:
Jesus on Leadership(60 minutes)

Preparation

- Gather the following items:
  - ❑ *Catholic Youth Bible*s or other Bibles, one for every three or four participants
  - ❑ copies of handout 9, "Leading As Jesus Did," one for each participant
  - ❑ pens or pencils
  - ❑ newsprint, one sheet for the leader plus one sheet for every three or four participants
  - ❑ markers, one for every three or four participants
  - ❑ masking tape
  - ❑ chairs and other props for role-plays
  - ❑ about twenty sheets of blank paper
  - ❑ copies of handout 10, "Jesus as Leader," one for each participant
  - ❑ self-stick notes, five for each participant
  - ❑ a tape player or a CD player
  - ❑ tapes and CDs of reflective instrumental music
- On a sheet of newsprint, list the following questions:
  - ○ Who are the characters in the story?
  - ○ Where is the action and what is happening?
  - ○ What is Jesus doing?
  - ○ When does the story take place?
  - ○ What qualities in Jesus have amazed or challenged people?
- Prepare a space in the room where the groups can perform role-plays. Have some chairs and other props available for use.
- On a sheet of newsprint, list the following questions:
  - ○ How did Jesus interact with people?
  - ○ Why did people flock to Jesus?
  - ○ What qualities or characteristics did Jesus possess?

News Report Role-Plays (30 minutes)

1. Welcome the participants and introduce the session using these comments:

- Many people are familiar with WWJD?—the slogan that stands for "What Would Jesus Do?"

- Today's session helps us look at what Jesus did as a leader in the many settings he encountered.
- We know that Jesus was a leader, but he never held an office, he never won an election, and he never had an official title next to his name.
- Jesus led others in the everyday situations in which he found himself. Today we will take some time to find out more about those situations and the leadership qualities and the principles by which Jesus led.

2. Form small groups of three or four participants. Give each group a Bible, and give each participant a copy of handout 9 and a pen or a pencil. Assign each group one of the Scripture passages listed on the handout. Then give this instruction:

- Read the assigned Scripture passage and talk about the questions listed on the handout. Choose someone from the group to record your answers to the questions.

3. After 5 minutes, post the list of five questions that you wrote on newsprint and give these instructions:

- Your small group is to prepare a news report based on the Scripture passage you just read. Select one person to play the role of the reporter. The rest of the group should portray people from the Scripture passage who witness what happens.
- Note the five questions I have posted on newsprint. These questions will give you more direction on what should be included in the news reports. You have 5 minutes to prepare your role-plays.

4. Invite the participants to gather in the area you have prepared for the presentation of the role-plays. Invite each group to present its role-play.

Jesus' Leadership Qualities (20 minutes)

1. Instruct the participants to return to their small groups, and to appoint one person to be the facilitator of the group. Give each group a sheet of newsprint and a marker. Post the list of three questions that you wrote on newsprint, and ask the small groups to share their responses to the questions. Tell them to write their responses to the last question on the newsprint you provided. Explain that they will have 5 minutes to work.

2. Gather the participants back together, and invite each small group to present its list of Jesus' qualities or characteristics to the large group. Post the small groups' responses on the wall so that all can see them. Then ask the participants this question:

- After seeing the news reports and spending time with your Scripture passage, what conclusions can you draw about Jesus as a leader?

As the participants share their responses out loud, write each answer on a sheet of blank paper—one answer to a sheet—large enough for others to see. Post all the sheets on a wall, slightly apart from one another.

3. Ask the participants this question:

- The answers listed on the handout tell us what Jesus did in his time and place. How can we act as Jesus did in our own time and place? Complete this sentence: "One who leads like Jesus will . . ."

As the participants share their responses out loud, write each answer on a sheet of blank paper—one answer to a sheet. Post all the sheets on the same wall as you did the responses in step 2.

4. Distribute handout 10. Talk about the information presented on the handout. Then ask:

- Did we miss anything that should be added to the responses listed on the wall?

Add any qualities or actions that the young people suggest. If the participants have overlooked a significant number of the qualities or actions listed on the handout, pause and talk more about those items.

Personal Leadership Reflection (10 minutes)

1. Give each participant five self-stick notes. Have everyone write their names on each note, then invite them to reflect on their own leadership qualities and their own style of leadership. Ask them to look at the posted qualities of ways that Jesus led. Play reflective instrumental music in the background, and give the participants about 3 minutes to reflect.

2. Ask the participants to take the self-stick notes on which they have recorded their names up to the wall and post them on qualities they have in common with Jesus and on actions they have done or want to do in the future. Explain that they must place their names on five different qualities and actions. Invite them to do this quietly and prayerfully. Continue to play reflective music.

3. Ask the following questions:

- How do you feel right now?
- What are you feeling challenged to do?

4. Summarize the session by making the following points:

- Jesus led people through his everyday actions. At times he did extraordinary things (miracles), but often he greatly affected people through simple actions—he listened, he was compassionate, he reached out to people in need.
- Jesus made a difference wherever he went, and we are called to do the same. That is what it means to lead as Jesus did.

- Leadership is not always easy. As leaders, we may be called to do or say something difficult.
- Leadership requires integrity. Though no one expects us to be perfect leaders, we can be expected to act with integrity, to choose what is right and good. Jesus experienced tough times in leadership too. Frequently his leadership was called into question. Jesus stayed true to his integrity and his knowledge of what was right and what was wrong.
- We are all blessed with gifts and abilities we can use for others.

Hearing the Call to Lead (10 minutes)

Preparation

- Gather the following items:
  - ❑ copies of handout 11, "Hearing the Call to Lead," one for each participant
  - ❑ copies of *Spirit & Song* or another hymnal, one for each participant
  - ❑ a *Catholic Youth Bible* or other Bible, marked at Jer. 1:4–8
- Select a gathering song and a closing song from the *Spirit & Song* Connections in this chapter, or from another hymnal.
- Ask a participant to proclaim the Scripture reading that is noted on handout 11.

    1. Invite the participants to gather for prayer, facing the wall that has been created with the qualities and actions of Jesus and their own names. Differentiate the sides of the room so that the young people know if they are on the left side or the right side. Give each participant a copy of handout 11 as well as a hymnal.

    2. Begin the prayer with the sign of the cross, and then lead the participants in singing the gathering song you have selected.

    3. Offer this opening prayer:

- Almighty God, you gave us your Son, Jesus, to show us what it means to lead and serve others. He washed the feet of his friends and never turned down anyone in need. We ask you to help us to be people who take our call to leadership seriously. We ask this through our Lord Jesus Christ, your Son, who lives and reigns with you and the Holy Spirit, one God forever and ever. Amen.

Spirit & Song connections

- ◆ "How Beautiful," by Twila Paris
- ◆ "Path of Life," by Trevor Thomson
- ◆ "The Summons," by John L. Bell and arranged by Bobby Fisher

4. Direct the volunteer to proclaim the Scripture reading. Allow a moment for quiet reflection. Then invite the participants to pray the response together as noted on the handout.

5. Lead the group in a blessing of one another. Invite the participants on the left side of the room to stand and extend their hands over their peers on the right side of the room. Read the five lines of blessing from the handout, one line at a time as noted, asking the participants to repeat each line after you. Then tell those on the left to sit down and those on the right to stand, and repeat the process.

6. Invite the participants to join in singing the closing song.

Options and Actions

- **Want ads.** Create a list of leadership opportunities available in your community, in local schools, or in the parish. Make sure that some of the opportunities are unofficial roles of service (for example, befriending people who are alone at school, volunteering at a nursing home, and helping an older neighbor). Urge the young people to think about ways they can use their gifts in making a difference.

- **Thank-you notes.** Ask the participants to list five people they know who exemplify one or more of Jesus' leadership styles or qualities. Ask them to write those people each a thank-you note in the coming weeks. Suggest the following format for the body of the note: "In my youth ministry program, I have been studying Jesus as a leader. One of the leadership qualities I see Jesus possessing is _____. I have noticed this quality in you when you _____. Thank you for being an example of Christian leadership. I too will try to follow Jesus, by _____."

Leading As Jesus Did

Scripture reading	Leadership qualities	Jesus as leader	Christian leaders
Matthew 21:12–17 (Jesus cleanses the temple.)	Principle centered	A person of principle	Lead lives based on the values and beliefs that they embrace: walk the talk
John 2:1–11 (The wedding at Cana)	Incorruptible	A person of integrity	Demonstrate integrity by being true to values in word and action
Matthew 5:1–12 (The Beatitudes)	Vision oriented	A visionary	Establish a vision that gives direction to all members
Matthew 22:15–22 (A question about paying taxes)	Proactive	A proactive person	Hold values that determine how they will act; do not react out of feelings and situations
Matthew 15:32–39 (Feeding the four thousand)	Compassionate	A person of compassion	Respond to the needs and pains of others
John 8:1–11 (A woman caught in adultery)	Forgiving	A forgiver of past transgressions	Forgive unconditionally while pointing to the future
Luke 10:38–42 (Jesus visits Martha and Mary.)	Listening	A listener	Listen to people and really try to hear their issues, concerns, and feelings
Mark 2:1–12 (Jesus heals a person who is paralyzed.)	Interdependent	Interdependent with God and others	Rely on God; rely on the gifts of the community to complement personal gifts and weaknesses
Matthew 10:5–15 (The mission of the Twelve)	Empowering	Empowering of others	Share power; know that God has the power; bring out the best in others; equip others with the skills needed to contribute
John 13:1–8,12–15 (Jesus washes the disciples' feet.)	Serving others	A servant-leader	Meet the needs of the people they lead; don't ask others to do what they themselves are not willing to do

Jesus as Leader

1. What did Jesus do or say in the passage?

2. How did the people in the story react to Jesus?

3. What qualities in Jesus might have amazed or challenged the people in the story?

Hearing the Call to Lead

Gather

Gathering Song

Opening Prayer

Listen

Scripture Reading

Jeremiah was a prophet called by God to challenge the Israelites to healthy and holy living. His prophecies brought hope to the people. Jeremiah was surprised that God called him to leadership. Yet Jeremiah followed through with God's desire for him and became a prophet leader during a time of trial. Listen to a reading from the Book of Jeremiah.

Read Jeremiah 1:4–8.

Respond

Right: Jesus, you taught us the meaning of leadership when you washed the feet of your friends.
Response (all): May we lead and love as you did.

Left: Jesus, you never turned down a request for help or healing.
Response (all): May we lead and love as you did.

Right: Jesus, you accepted all people and challenged them to be their best selves.
Response (all): May we lead and love as you did.

Left: Jesus, you call us as Christian leaders to meet the needs of our families, our friends, and our communities.
Response (all): May we lead and love as you did.

Send Forth

Blessing of Leaders

God, we call upon you to bless the work of these hands, these hearts,
and these minds.

Bless in a special way our friends who have been called to leadership.

Give them courage to act with justice, and make decisions for the good
of all.

Bless each one of them with your love and presence.

We ask this through Christ our Lord. Amen.

Closing Song

Study It

Core Session:
Unexpected Leaders
(55 minutes)

◆ The Election
  (25 minutes)
◆ Biblical Connections
  (20 minutes)
◆ A Personal Reflection
  (10 minutes)

Pray It

◆ Are You Listening?
  (10 minutes)

Live It

◆ Acknowledging leaders

8 Unexpected Leaders of the Bible

Overview

The Bible is filled with stories about people called to leadership who did not want the job or who even seemed ill prepared to do the things they were called to do. This session helps the young people talk about the skills, talents, and strengths they believe are necessary for leadership, and invites them to recognize the ways God calls many people to leadership, sometimes in spite of their natural abilities. The session uses biblical characters to help the participants recognize different styles of leadership and the humanness of the people God has called throughout history.

Outcomes

◆ The participants will become aware of biblical figures who served as leaders.
◆ The participants will be challenged to think differently about what makes someone a good leader.
◆ The participants will be invited to explore ways they can use their gifts to be leaders in the Church and in the world.

Core Session:
Unexpected Leaders (55 minutes)

Preparation

- Gather the following items:
  - ❑ copies of handout 12, "Election Notes," one for each participant
  - ❑ pens or pencils
  - ❑ copies of handout 13, "Student Council Ballot," one for each participant plus one for every five or six participants
  - ❑ newsprint and markers
  - ❑ masking tape
  - ❑ copies of handout 14, "Biblical Connections," one for each participant
  - ❑ *Catholic Youth Bible*s or other Bibles, one for every five or six participants
  - ❑ copies of handout 15, "God Qualifies the Called," one for each participant
  - ❑ a tape player or a CD player
  - ❑ tapes or CDs of reflective instrumental music
- Prepare and post a sheet of newsprint that lists the names of the fourteen candidates noted on handout 13.
- Write the following questions on a sheet of newsprint and post the newsprint where all can see it:
  - ○ What made this person a good leader?
  - ○ What made this person an unlikely leader?
  - ○ Why did God call this person?
  - ○ Why did this person say yes?

The Election (25 minutes)

1. Gather the participants into a large group. Begin with the following comments:

- It is not uncommon for us to choose leaders. We choose a president every four years, as well as state and local leaders, and you have probably been involved in selecting class officers, presidents of clubs you belong to, or chairs of certain committees.

• Today we are going to look at what makes someone a good leader. Is it natural abilities, certain qualities, or specific skills? Does a person need all those qualities and skills to lead effectively? Is it possible to lead without them?

2. Distribute handout 12, and pens or pencils. Share the following ideas:

• Imagine that your school is holding a student council election today. As a responsible member of your class, you want to make an educated decision about who should be elected. You are a junior in high school, and you want to make sure your senior year will be a good one.

• Without talking to anyone, read the information on the handout and begin to decide who will make the best leaders for your school.

• As you are reading, I will give each of you a ballot [handout 13]. You will need to select seven people to serve on the student council. You have about 5 minutes to read the notes on the handout and make your selections on the ballot.

3. Ask the participants to form small groups of five or six. Provide each group with an additional copy of handout 13. Give the following instructions:

• As a group, your job is to agree on seven people who should lead your school.

• You have 10 minutes to talk with one another and come to a group decision about who should be selected as the leaders of your school.

4. Call time after 10 minutes, even if the groups are not done. It is more important to process their conversation than it is to have them come to a decision.

Gather the participants into a large group, and ask each small group to tell who it selected as leaders. As the small groups report, place a check mark next to each selected name on the posted list of candidates. Summarize the balloting by noting who received many votes and who received few or none. There is no need to declare a winner of this election; you might need to refocus the participants' attention on learning more about leadership through this activity than on declaring the winners of the election.

5. Ask the following questions, recording the answers to the first question on newsprint:

• What criteria did you use in making your decisions?

• Why did you choose those criteria?

• If someone does not meet those criteria, do you think they can lead? Why or why not?

6. Make the following comments, using information from the discussion in step 5:

- We can sometimes be too narrow in our thinking about who can be a leader.
- We have seen, throughout the ages, that some people are great at leading in one way, but not as successful in other ways.
- For example, Jimmy Carter has achieved many great things since leaving the U.S. presidency. He has become one of the most trusted leaders in the world, and he has made an incredible difference in the lives of thousands through his volunteer work and his international efforts to create peaceful and humane conditions. However, when he was president, many people considered him ineffective.
- Sometimes the people who look least like a "classic leader" are those who make the biggest difference for good in our world.
- There are young people who would never think about putting themselves up for a student council election at their schools, but who do incredibly good things in their parishes and in their communities. [Name some young people who do good things without the benefit of an official position. Invite the participants to offer names as well.]
- We are now going to take a closer look at the candidates from the student council elections.

Biblical Connections (20 minutes)

1. Distribute handout 14. Reveal the biblical connections to the candidates on the ballot. Ask the participants whether they had guessed at the connections.

2. Invite the participants to return to their small groups. Assign one or more of the biblical characters to each group. You might select some that received many votes and some that received few or no votes during the group-reporting process. Give each group a copy of the *CYB* and the following instructions:

- Your group is to read the Scripture passage and the *CYB* article about your assigned biblical character or characters.
- For each character, answer the four questions noted on the newsprint. [Refer the participants to the newsprint you have prepared and read the questions out loud.]

Give the groups about 10 minutes to work. While they are working, provide each group with a sheet of newsprint and a couple of markers.

3. Invite the groups each to create a poster about leadership. Ask them to include anything they have learned during this session about leadership and who is called to leadership. Tell them they have 5 minutes to create their posters.

4. Gather all the participants together. Ask each group to share its poster.

5. Draw conclusions such as these from the poster presentation:

- God did not give every person every gift. We are called to use the natural abilities we have in order to do good in this world. We all contribute differently.

- Each of us is called to live our faith in this world, and if we trust, God will ensure that we have what we need to accomplish this work.

- The characters from the Bible were able to accomplish great things even though they were very "human" (had lots of faults and weaknesses), because they answered when God called and were willing to follow God's will. How ready are you to answer God's call?

A Personal Reflection (10 minutes)

1. Distribute handout 15. Invite each person to think about the passages on the handout and to answer the reflection questions. Play reflective instrumental music softly in the background, and give the participants about 7 minutes to write and pray.

2. Conclude the session by inviting the young people to gather in the prayer space with their written reflections.

Are You Listening? (10 minutes)

Preparation

- Gather the following items:
  - ❑ a *Catholic Youth Bible* or other Bible, marked at 1 Sam. 3:1–19
  - ❑ a candle and matches
  - ❑ a cloth
  - ❑ a tape player or a CD player
  - ❑ tapes and CDs of reflective instrumental music
  - ❑ copies of *Spirit & Song* or another hymnal, one for each participant
- Designate a prayer space by placing the Bible and the candle on the cloth on the floor. The participants should have enough room to sit on the floor in a circle around the cloth.

- Invite one of the participants to proclaim the Scripture passage.
- Select a closing song from the *Spirit & Song* Connections in this session, or any song with a theme that reflects trust in God.

1. Gather the participants in the prayer space, recruit a participant to light the candle, and begin the prayer with the sign of the cross.

2. Invite the volunteer to proclaim the Scripture reading. Allow a moment for quiet reflection.

3. Pray the following words:

- Gracious and loving God, you have gifted us with many talents; you have touched our hearts. Today we pause for a moment to ask you to speak to each of us. We pray for the help we need to do your will.

Play reflective instrumental music and pause for 5 minutes to allow private prayer. Invite the participants to look at handout 15 and to pray for the things they listed for the last question on the handout.

4. Pray the petitions listed here, inviting the participants to respond to each by saying, "God, we thank you."

- For the talents and the abundance of gifts that are ours . . .
- For the faith that stirs and grows in our hearts . . .
- For the many people who have been instruments of goodness in our lives . . .

5. Pray the following petitions, inviting the participants to respond to each by saying, "God, help us to trust you."

- When fear rises up in us and we do not believe in ourselves . . .
- When busyness and pressures lead us to lose the sense of you within us . . .
- When emptiness, loneliness, and other struggles block out your love for us . . .

6. Pray the following petitions, inviting the participants to respond to each by saying, "God of love, dwell within us."

- As we grow in believing in our goodness . . .
- As we allow more and more of ourselves to be influenced by your presence . . .
- As we seek to discern how and when to share our goodness with others . . .

7. Conclude by inviting the participants to join in singing the closing song you selected.

Mediaconnections

- ◆ *Patch Adams* (Universal Studios, 116 minutes, 1998, rated PG-13). This movie is about a troubled man who finds his call in serving others as a doctor.
- ◆ *Simon Birch* (Hollywood Pictures, 113 minutes, 1998, rated PG). This movie deals with an un-likely leader who believes that God has called him for a higher purpose.
- ◆ *Veggie Tales: Heroes of the Bible—Lions, Shepherds, and Queens (Oh My!)* (Warner Home Videos, 75 minutes, 2003, rated G). This movie introduces heroes of the Bible through cartoons and songs.

LiVE it!

Options and Actions

- **Acknowledging leaders.** Invite the participants to write notes or e-mails to a few people in the parish or community whom they consider great leaders. Those might be people who do not get a lot of recognition for the good that they do.

Election Notes

- **Alfredo** recently disowned his rich parents. He doesn't talk a lot because he has a speech impediment. When he does speak, he can be really demanding. His younger brother does most of the talking for him. Alfredo was on the cross-country team this year.
- **Ellie** is really nice, but she can't be involved in many school activities because she has to work at the family restaurant. Surprisingly, she dates the captain of the football team. His friends don't like her.
- **Jerry** skipped a grade and is younger than you and your classmates. He spends a lot of time in detention and hangs out with the troublemakers. He's kind of a loudmouth, always telling others how to be better people. His teachers are always trying to get him to be on the debate team, but he is afraid to do something so public.
- **Tanisha** is on the varsity basketball team and is a little feisty. She fouls out of the game often. She's a little bossy and judgmental.
- **Henry** plays on the chess team. He's somewhat of a pushover. It is commonly known that his girlfriend cheats on him. She broke up with him once because she wanted to date someone else, and he begged her to get back together with him. When he isn't with her, he spends a lot of time at home.
- **Anjali** lives with her stepmother. Neither of her parents is in the picture. She doesn't stand out in the crowd. She is very loyal to the few friends she has.
- **Jorge** joined the fishing club, but he quit after he fell out of the boat on the first outing. He's also well remembered because at a football game he scored the winning touchdown . . . for the other team. He quit that team too. He seems to have trouble sticking with commitments.
- **Judy** has courage and a lot of faith in herself. This year she really had people talking because she made the wrestling team. Many people didn't approve. She was successful and beat last year's state champion. Many people aren't sure how to take her. She doesn't seem to have a lot of friends.
- **Chuyen** got into a fight with a senior who was a real bully, when he was a freshman. The senior was a state-winning weightlifter, and Chuyen managed to win by outsmarting him. Chuyen is the youngest of a big family. He recently started dating a girl who was already dating someone else. This caused a lot of gossip.

- **Maggie** has a bad reputation. You are not sure how true the rumors you have heard about her are. She is the leader of the feminist club at school. She also seems to be present at important school events.
- **Mariette** is a quiet, humble person. She shocked everyone in your class when she had a baby during her first year of high school. Most people don't know her well, mostly because they don't know what to say to her.
- **Matt** is the class bookie. He takes bets on all the school games. He has a history of not being real nice to the people who lose their bets to him.
- **Fabian** crusades for causes. He is pro-choice and lets everyone know it. He is critical and judgmental of anyone who disagrees with him. He also follows all school rules and feels that rules are very important to have.
- **Juan** tends to drive you crazy. He always asks the dumbest questions in class, and you and your classmates are usually frustrated with him. He likes to fish with his dad often, and he is always talking about fishing.

Student Council Ballot

Choose seven candidates to serve on the student council.

☐ Alfredo	☐ ~~Judy~~
☐ Ellie	☐ Chuyen
☐ Jerry	☐ Maggie
☐ Tanisha	☐ Mariette
☐ Henry	☐ Matt
☐ Anjali	☐ Fabian
☐ Jorge	☐ Juan

Biblical Connections

Candidate	Biblical character	Bible passage	*The Catholic Youth Bible* article
Alfredo	Moses	Exodus 4:10–17	"Introducing Moses"
Ellie	Esther	Esther 2:15–18, chapters 7–8	"The Book of Esther: In Depth"
Jerry	Jeremiah	Jeremiah 1:4–10	"Introducing Jeremiah"
Tanisha	Deborah	Judges, chapter 4	"Wartime Women"
Henry	Hosea	Hosea 3:1–5	"The Book of Hosea: In Depth"
Anjali	Ruth	Ruth 2:1–16	"The Book of Ruth: In Depth"
Jorge	Jonah	Jonah, chapter 1	"The Book of Jonah: In Depth"
Judy	Judith	Judith, chapter 8	"The Book of Judith: In Depth"
Chuyen	David	1 Samuel 16:1–13, 17:33–51	"Introducing David"
Maggie	Mary Magdalene	Luke 8:1–3, 24:1–11	"Introducing Mary Magdalene"
Mariette	Blessed Virgin Mary	Luke 1:26–38	"Introducing Mary of Nazareth"
Matt	Matthew	Matthew 9:9–13	"The Gospel According to Matthew: In Depth"
Fabian	Paul	Acts 7:54—8:3, 9:1–19	"Introducing Saint Paul"
Juan	Peter	Matthew 15:13–20	"Introducing Peter the Rock"

God Qualifies the Called

Scripture Passages

Pause for a moment and reflect on these words from the Scriptures:

> Now to him who by the power at work within us is able to accomplish abundantly far more than we can ask or imagine, to him be glory in the church and in Christ Jesus to all generations, forever and ever. Amen. (Ephesians 3:20–21)

> I am confident of this, that the one who began a good work among you will bring it to completion by the day of Jesus Christ. . . . And this is my prayer, that your love may overflow more and more with knowledge and full insight to help you to determine what is best, so that in the day of Christ you may be pure and blameless, having produced the harvest of righteousness that comes through Jesus Christ for the glory and praise of God. (Phillippians 1:6,9–11)

> Let no one despise your youth, but set the believers an example in your speech and conduct, in love, in faith, in purity. Until I arrive, give attention to the public reading of scripture, to exhortation, to teaching. Do not neglect the gift that is in you, which was given to you through prophecy with the laying on of hands by the council of elders. Put these things into practice, devote yourself to them, so that all may see your progress. Pay close attention to yourself and to your teaching; continue in these things, for in doing this you will save both yourself and your hearers. (1 Timothy 4:11–16)

Reflection Questions

Answer these questions in writing.

What are you naturally good at doing? (Think broadly. Listening is as important as singing; caring for others is as important as having athletic ability.)

How have you used your gifts for the good of others?

How could you use your gifts, talents, and energy for others?

What might God be calling you to do?

What would you need from God to feel more confident?

9 Naming and Claiming Gifts in Self and Others

AT A GLANCE

Pray It

◆ God Gifts Us
(5 minutes)

Study It

Core Session: Naming and Claiming Gifts in Self and Others (45 minutes)

◆ Naming and Claiming My Gifts—Self-Reflection
(10 minutes)

◆ Naming the Gifts in Others
(25 minutes)

◆ Called, Gifted, and Sent
(10 minutes)

Live It

◆ Gifts from the heart

Overview

Young people need safe environments to explore their giftedness and affirm their own gifts and those of others. This session provides an opportunity for naming and claiming gifts. The task may be intimidating for some young people. For that reason, creating a safe environment is important so that the participants can genuinely enter into the activities. This session works best when the group has had some history of working together, because it requires the participants to name the gifts they see in themselves and in others.

Outcomes

◆ The participants will name their own gifts.
◆ The participants will identify the gifts of others.

Background Reading

◆ Scriptural connections: Psalm 139 (the inescapable God), Matt. 25:14–30 (the parable of the ten bridesmaids), Luke 10:1–4 (the mission of the seventy)
◆ *Catholic Youth Bible* article connections: "The Principle of *Kuumba*" (Matt. 25:14–30), "Spice Me Up, Lord" (Luke 14:34–35), "A Little Goes a Long Way" (John 6:1–14)

God Gifts Us (5 minutes)

Preparation

- Gather the following items:
  - ❑ chairs
  - ❑ a low table, a cloth, and a cross
  - ❑ a tape player or a CD player
  - ❑ tapes or CDs of reflective instrumental music
  - ❑ a *Catholic Youth Bible* or other Bible, marked at Ps. 139:1–18
  - ❑ copies of handout 16, "We Are Fearfully and Wonderfully Made," one for each participant
- Set up the room by placing the chairs in a circle, with the table in the middle (use a low table so that it does not obstruct the participants' views of one another). Place the cloth and the cross on the table.
- Invite a participant to proclaim the Scripture reading.

1. As the participants arrive, play reflective instrumental music softly and welcome them. Distribute handout 16. Begin with a moment of silence, followed by the sign of the cross. Then pray:

- Open our hearts and our minds that we may worthily hear your word and live it.

2. Invite the volunteer to proclaim the Scripture reading. Allow a moment of quiet reflection.

3. Ask the participants to turn to the handout. Divide the group into a left side and a right side. Have each side pray the prayer as indicated on the handout. Lead everyone in praying the response after each phrase.

4. Close by praying:

- God of goodness, you gift each of us in unique ways. Give us courage to name and claim our gifts so that through them we can serve you and our world. We ask this through Jesus our Lord. Amen.

Spirit & Song connections

- "Gather Your People," by Bob Hurd, with harmony by Craig Kingsbury
- "This Little Light of Mine" (traditional spiritual)
- "We Are Called to Serve," by Julie Smith and Tim Smith
- "We Are God's People," by Jeffrey Roscoe
- "We Are God's Work of Art," by Mark Friedman

Core Session: Naming and Claiming Gifts in Self and Others (45 minutes)

Preparation

- Gather the following items:
  - ❑ copies of handout 17, "My Gifts," one for each participant
  - ❑ pens or pencils
  - ❑ a hole punch
  - ❑ sheets of construction paper, cut in half, one half-sheet for each participant
  - ❑ a skein of yarn or a roll of string
- Punch two holes in each half-sheet of construction paper, one on each top corner, and attach a piece of yarn or string to the paper by threading the ends through the holes and tying knots. The participants will be asked to place the resulting necklaces around their necks—the construction paper should hang to their chests.

Naming and Claiming My Gifts—Self-Reflection (10 minutes)

1. Introduce the session by saying:
- Naming and claiming our own gifts can be challenging. We are often very critical of ourselves. During this session we will focus on the giftedness of ourselves and of others.
- This will be a very reflective session.
- The word *gift* describes many things. Sometimes we talk about a person's natural abilities, talents, or specific skills. In the Church we recognize that each of us has a special charism—gift of the Holy Spirit—given to us for the good of the community. All those things we will talk about as gifts today, because regardless of why we are good at something—we learned how, it comes naturally, or we practiced for many years—we each have gifts we can share with others.

2. Form small groups of four or five participants. Distribute handout 17, and pens or pencils. Then offer the following instructions:
- I invite you to begin by reflecting on your own gifts. Review the handout and check off each gift you believe you possess.

TryThis

If the participants know one another well, have the members of the small groups name one another's gifts. Tape a piece of construction paper on each participant's back. Invite the participants to write the gift or gifts they see in a person on that person's paper. When everyone has at least five gifts on their papers, invite them to take the piece of papers off their backs and add other gifts they possess.

3. After 3 minutes say:

- Now narrow your list to your top ten gifts. Circle those ten gifts.

4. After 3 minutes say:

- Continue to narrow your list so that you have five gifts. Put a box around those gifts.

While the participants are completing this step, distribute the construction paper "necklaces."

5. After 3 minutes say:

- Write your top five gifts on the construction paper. Once you have done that, place the construction paper around your neck.

6. Ask the participants to take turns sharing the five gifts listed on their construction paper with the people in their small groups.

Naming the Gifts in Others (25 minutes)

1. Say:

- Each small group will now become an affirmation circle.
- One at a time, each person in your small group will be asked to sit in the middle of the circle to share her or his gifts, and to hear feedback from the rest of the group.
- This is an opportunity to affirm one another's giftedness. Please use positive, concrete examples to share how you see the specific gifts lived out in each person in your small group.
- Please share your insights in a respectful manner.
- The person sitting in the middle will name out loud the gifts listed on his or her piece of construction paper.
- A moment of silence will follow, to allow reflection on that person's giftedness.
- After the silence each participant should share examples of how she or he sees the gifts of that person being lived out.
- Once everyone has had an opportunity to speak, a new person will move to the middle and the process will begin again.
- Are there any questions? [Pause and respond to questions.]
- You may begin.

2. After 3 or 4 minutes, invite another person to sit in the middle, and continue this process until everyone has been affirmed.

Called, Gifted, and Sent (10 minutes)

1. Regather into a large group and offer the following explanation:

- Each us is uniquely gifted by God. There is no one else like us, with our life story, our gifts, our treasures.

- Today you have had an opportunity to name your gifts and to have them affirmed by others.

- The gifts we have been given also come with responsibilities.

- Christian leaders know they have been called by God and gifted in unique ways in order to transform the world for goodness.

- Through Baptism God claims us for his own. When we were baptized, the priest said these words: "Father, God of mercy, through these waters of baptism you have filled us with new life as your very own children" (*The Rite of Baptism for Children,* p. 38). We become sons and daughters of God. If we are attentive enough, throughout our life we will hear God's voice calling us—always calling us to love, to goodness, to justice, and to peace.

- We are called by God, we are gifted by God, and we are sent by God to transform the world.

- Jesus had a vision of a peaceful, loving, kind, just world. The great call is to join with the millions who have gone before us to bring that vision to reality. In Baptism the celebrant says, "You call those who have been baptized to announce the Good News of Jesus Christ to people everywhere" (*Rite of Baptism,* p. 39).

2. Invite the participants to look at their gift lists and narrow them down to their three main gifts. Ask them to place a star next to each of those three gifts.

3. Pray the following words:

- Loving God, you have formed us in our mother's womb, you who know our sitting and our standing, you who gift us. We thank you for calling us through our Baptism to share our gifts with the world. We offer our gifts to you as we claim them as our own by naming them aloud.

4. Starting to your right, invite the participants in turn to share their top three gifts. Say something like this:

- We offer our gifts of . . .

5. Conclude the session by praying the Lord's Prayer together.

Familyconnections

◆ Invite the participants to make small hearts for their family members, and follow the Live It activity "Gifts from the Heart" with their families.

◆ Suggest that the participants hold an affirmation circle with their families. Encourage them to follow the same process that was used in the session.

Mediaconnections

◆ *Harry Potter and the Chamber of Secrets* (Warner Home Video, 161 minutes, 2002, rated PG). Harry learns he has a special gift—but he fears what it means in his life.

◆ *The Lion King* (Disney Studios, 88 minutes, 1994, rated G). Simba discovers that he must use his unique gifts for the good of others.

◆ *The Wizard of Oz* (Warner Studios, 101 minutes, 1939, rated G). Dorothy and the others discover they have the gifts they have always desired.

LIVE it!

Options and Actions

• **Gifts from the heart.** Give each participant ten small hearts made of construction paper. Invite them to think of ten significant people in their lives. Ask them to write on each heart the name of one person and one gift they admire in that person. Encourage the participants to give out or mail the hearts to those people during the next week.

We Are Fearfully and Wonderfully Made

Response (all): **We praise you because we are fearfully and wonderfully made.**

Left: Each one of us is made in your image and likeness. Within us we find your goodness, your compassion, and your love. Teach us to be in touch with those great qualities within ourselves.

Response (all): **We praise you because we are fearfully and wonderfully made.**

Right: Each one of us is unique. You have blessed each of us with wonderful gifts. Teach us to accept our gifts, rejoice in our gifts, and find ways to nurture our gifts.

Response (all): **We praise you because we are fearfully and wonderfully made.**

Left: We look around us and marvel at the gifts of others. Grant us courage to celebrate those gifts. Give us the words to genuinely affirm one another's gifts.

Response (all): **We praise you because we are fearfully and wonderfully made.**

Right: We look around us and see a world ready to tear us down, a world filled with comparisons and competition. Grant us the courage to stand up against this world by supporting one another and by building a community strengthened through our unique gifts.

Response (all): **We praise you because we are fearfully and wonderfully made.**

Left: Help us to move forward together. Open our hearts and our minds to the gifts of others. Challenge us to embrace diversity so that we can learn from the wisdom of those we encounter.

Response (all): **We praise you because we are fearfully and wonderfully made.**

Right: Open our hearts and our minds to see you in every person we serve. Challenge us to live out the Gospel call to share our gifts with the world and to unite with others in building your Reign here on earth.

Response (all): **We praise you because we are fearfully and wonderfully made. Amen.**

My Gifts

- [ ] art
- [ ] building consensus
- [ ] camping
- [ ] caring
- [ ] children's activities
- [ ] clerical work
- [ ] coaching
- [ ] communicating
- [ ] community outreach
- [ ] computer skills
- [ ] cooking
- [ ] coordinating events
- [ ] craft making
- [ ] dancing
- [ ] delegating
- [ ] drama
- [ ] education
- [ ] empathizing
- [ ] encouraging others
- [ ] environmentalism

- [ ] evaluating programs
- [ ] evangelizing
- [ ] facilitating groups
- [ ] faith
- [ ] finance or business
- [ ] friendship
- [ ] fund-raising
- [ ] humor
- [ ] intelligence
- [ ] joy
- [ ] kindness
- [ ] languages
- [ ] leading
- [ ] leading small groups
- [ ] library work
- [ ] listening
- [ ] liturgy
- [ ] loyalty
- [ ] love

- [ ] maintenance work
- [ ] mediation
- [ ] motivation
- [ ] music
- [ ] negotiation
- [ ] nonviolence
- [ ] offering time
- [ ] operating sound systems
- [ ] organizing
- [ ] patience
- [ ] peacemaking
- [ ] performing
- [ ] persistence
- [ ] photography
- [ ] planning
- [ ] praying
- [ ] public speaking
- [ ] recruiting others
- [ ] repairing

- [ ] researching
- [ ] selling
- [ ] serving others
- [ ] sewing
- [ ] sharing new ideas
- [ ] social justice
- [ ] sports
- [ ] supporting
- [ ] teaching
- [ ] team building
- [ ] videography
- [ ] visiting others
- [ ] working hard
- [ ] working with the elderly
- [ ] writing
- [ ] youth ministry
- [ ] using my hands
- [ ] using tools
- [ ] other:

10 Communication Skills

AT A GLANCE

Study It

**Core Session:
Communication Skills
(60 minutes)**

- A Picture Says
  a Thousand Words
  (15 minutes)
- Play Ball
  (10 minutes)
- Roadblock Role-Plays
  (25 minutes)
- Ten Commandments of
  Communication
  (10 minutes)

Pray It

- Listening to God
  (5 minutes)

Overview

Learning more about the process of communication is essential for leaders—whether they have an up-front role within a group or they are going to use their gifts in service to friends, to family, or as members of a group. This session invites the participants to explore the process of communication as well as strategies for improving listening and communication skills.

Outcomes

- The participants will visualize how communication happens.
- The participants will witness roadblocks to communication and brainstorm solutions to those roadblocks.

Background Reading

- *Catholic Youth Bible* article connections: "Eli Teaches Samuel How to Pray" (1 Sam. 3:1–19), "A Prayer of Understanding" (Josh. 22:13–20)

Core Session: Communication Skills (60 minutes)

Preparation

- Gather the following items:
  - ❑ copies of resource 1, "A Picture Says a Thousand Words," one for every twenty-four participants
  - ❑ sheets of blank paper, two for every six to eight participants
  - ❑ pens or pencils
  - ❑ markers
  - ❑ masking tape
  - ❑ two foam balls (or two beanbags)
  - ❑ one copy of resource 2, "A Communication Process"
  - ❑ copies of resource 3, "Roadblocks to Effective Communication," one for each participant, plus one extra copy for every thirty participants
  - ❑ newsprint
- Secretly ask a participant to help you with the "Play Ball" activity. Explain that the second activity in this session is going to involve young people playing catch. The volunteer's job is to jump up and hit the ball so that the receiver cannot catch it. Show the volunteer the directions for the activity so that she or he knows when to jump up and cause a distraction.
- Cut apart the copies of resource 1 as scored. You will need one image from the resource for every small group of six to eight participants. If you have more than eight groups, give multiple groups the same picture. If your group is larger than thirty, enlarge the pictures so that each one is 8½ by 11 inches, to help the groups see the pictures when they are hung on a wall.
- Enlarge the diagram from resource 2 on a sheet of newsprint or an overhead projection.
- Cut apart the extra copies of resource 3 so that you have twelve slips of paper from each copy, with one roadblock on each slip.

A Picture Says a Thousand Words (15 minutes)

1. Welcome the participants, and introduce the session with these comments:

- Many people learn how to be good speakers by taking public-speaking classes or joining a debate team or a drama club, but often people do not take the time to really explore the process of communication.
- Today we will look at the process of communication and find out some ways we can better listen to and respond to others.

2. Organize the participants into small groups of six to eight. Have the groups gather in such a way that they will not be able to see what the other groups are working on. Give each group an image from resource 1, a sheet of blank paper, and a pen or a pencil. Announce this instruction:

- Each group has 5 minutes to write the directions that another group will need in order to draw the picture it is looking at. You are not allowed to draw anything on your paper—you can only use words. Are there any questions? [Pause and address any questions.] Begin the activity.

3. Ask the groups each to choose a name for themselves and to put that name on their finished directions. Then collect all the directions from the groups. Each group should keep its image. Mix up the directions, and redistribute them so that each group gets a different group's directions. Give the groups each a new sheet of paper and a marker, and tell them someone in each group should draw the picture described in the directions with the help of the rest of the group. Allow the groups 5 minutes to complete this part of the activity.

4. Collect the pictures and the directions from the groups. Post the groups' pictures on a wall. As each picture goes up, ask the group that wrote the directions for it to bring its original picture up front and hang it above the one drawn by the participants. (The group name on the directions will let you know which group has the original picture.)

5. If you have fewer than thirty participants, discuss the following questions as a large group. If you have more than thirty people, you might wish to have them discuss the questions in the small groups they worked in, or to divide the whole group into two or more groups for discussion.

- How confident did you feel when you were drawing your picture?
- How did you feel when you were writing your directions?
- How accurate was your drawing?
- What made this activity difficult?
- What does this activity illustrate about the challenges of good communication?

6. Summarize this activity by commenting on the ideas of the young people from the last question in step 5. You may wish to add or emphasize points like these:

- Communication is a process—one person is trying to say something and another person is trying to hear it, but what is said is not always understood.
- This activity shows that communication can sometimes be difficult.
- We rely on body language, visuals, tone of voice, and facial gestures to let us know more than words alone can say. It is important to pay attention to the whole message by looking at or paying attention to the person who is speaking.

Play Ball (10 minutes)

1. Invite the participants to gather as a large group, and ask two people who are good at playing catch to step forward. Tell one volunteer player to stand on one side of the group and the other player to stand on the other side of the group. (They will throw a ball over the heads of the other participants.) Make sure the secret volunteer you selected is in a position where he or she can jump up and hit the ball away. Give a foam ball (or a beanbag) to one of the players, and ask the two players to throw the ball back and forth.

2. As the players are throwing the ball back and forth, present the following information:

- The two volunteers are illustrating the communication process right now.
- The one throwing the ball is the sender, and the one catching the ball is the receiver. The ball is the message. The two volunteers switch between being the sender and being the receiver.
- When one person catches the ball and returns it, most often that person is giving the sender some feedback about what has been said.
- Feedback is a reaction, verbal or nonverbal, that communicates the receiver's interpretation of the message.

3. Ask for two more volunteers, and add them to the game of catch. Add another ball. As the four volunteers are throwing the two balls, present the following information:

- What we have here is a conversation that involves a number of different people as well as a number of different messages. When a lot of sending and receiving is going on, it is easier to drop the ball sometimes, or miss what someone is saying.

4. At this time the secret volunteer should jump up and try to misdirect the balls. When a ball drops out, before starting it into play again, present the following comments:

- Things sometimes disrupt a conversation, or distract us. What are some distractions that arise during conversations? [Collect some answers from the group.]
- For the process of communication to succeed, we need to eliminate as many distractions as possible.

5. Ask the volunteers to start playing catch again, and this time to try to have an actual conversation. Explain that every time they throw the ball, they have to speak a message to the person they are throwing the ball to, so that the ball symbolically carries the message to the person who catches it. Allow this to happen for about 1 minute.

6. Conclude this activity by making the following points:

- In conversation, just as in the game of catch, it is best when the messages we send get returned to us in a way that indicates they were understood. It is not fun to play catch with someone who is really bad at catching or throwing—when we do, we spend a lot of time chasing balls and standing around. But just like learning to catch and throw, learning to communicate takes some practice!
- Although not all our conversations involve a ball, they do involve something passing between us and other people. For our messages to be understood, someone must receive them. If no one hears a message, it drops out of the conversation, the same as when no one catches a ball, it hits the floor and stays there.
- In some conversations so many messages are being thrown around at the same time that it is impossible to catch all of them or to give feedback to the person trying to communicate.
- Communication begins with an idea. In this diagram [refer to the enlargement of the diagram from resource 2], you see that the girl has an idea. She is the sender, and she uses a collection of words to communicate that idea to the receiver.
- Even if the receiver, this boy, hears the words correctly, he may not understand the meaning intended by the sender. That is why it is important for a receiver to give feedback (to respond) to a sender—to see if the receiver understands the message in the way the sender intended.

Roadblock Role-Plays (25 minutes)

1. Give each participant a copy of resource 3. Using the resource and the enlargement of the diagram from resource 2, make the following presentation:

- We sometimes say things that halt a conversation. Doing so is similar to jumping up and sending a ball offtrack in a game of catch. Roadblocks are things we do (most often unintentionally) that stop a conversation from continuing on its natural path.

2. Draw a bold line between the two communicators on the diagram. Then continue as follows:

- Roadblocks are divided into three categories. Four roadblocks fall into the category of things that judge another person.
- If you look at number 4 on the resource, you will see that sometimes praising another person can be a roadblock. For example, if someone is really upset about a test they just took, it would be a roadblock to say, "You never do bad on tests, and you're so smart."
- Sending solutions can be a roadblock when the person who is speaking is not ready to hear solutions, or is not done telling you about the situation. To say "You ought to do this . . ." before you know all the details communicates to the person that you are done listening and want to get to the end of the conversation.
- Another category of roadblocks is things that avoid another's concern. The last roadblock, number 12, is often used: "Don't worry, everything will be okay." It does not make the person feel any better, nor does it give the person permission to continue to talk to you about the problem or situation. It ends the conversation.

3. Ask the participants to get into groups of about ten. Give a different roadblock cut from resource 3 to each of four participants in every group, making sure that each group gets at least one roadblock from each of the three categories on the resource. Then say:

- In your groups, you are to have a conversation about what you think are the most important communication skills.
- Those of you who have been given a slip of paper, your role is to try to roadblock the conversation by using the roadblock you have been assigned. You do not need to be obnoxious about your roadblocks!
- Everyone else in the group, try to have a good conversation, participating as you normally would.
- Choose someone who is not roadblocking to lead the discussion.
- Are there are any questions? [Address any questions.]
- Okay, begin. After 5 minutes I will call time.

4. Lead the participants in a discussion using the following questions:
- How did you feel during the conversation?
- What makes roadblocks difficult?
- Did the roadblocks in this conversation make you think of times when you roadblocked in other discussions? Explain.

TryThis

If you have fewer than twenty people, you can form two groups and use what is called a fishbowl process for step 3. Ask one group to conduct its conversation (to be the fish in the bowl), while the other group gathers around, looking in and listening (watch the fish in the bowl). Then switch groups. Note that this will take 10 minutes instead of 5.

5. Invite the groups to continue to talk about important communication skills, this time working to avoid roadblocking. Give them another 5 minutes to talk. Then ask these questions:
- How did you feel during the conversation?
- What are the differences between the two conversations?

6. Post these questions on newsprint:
- Which of the roadblocks on the resource do I use most often?
- What can I change about the way that I communicate with people?
- Which of the roadblocks on the resource do I experience from other people? Is there something I can do to help them not use roadblocks anymore?

Close this activity by inviting the participants to take a few minutes to reflect on the questions. Suggest that they use the back of the resource for responding to the questions.

Ten Commandments of Communication (10 minutes)

1. With the participants staying in their groups from the preceding activity, "Roadblock Role-Plays," give each group two sheets of newsprint and some markers. Direct each group to divide in half for the next activity. Ask the new groups to use what they learned from their conversation in the role-play activity, to come up with a list titled "Ten Commandments of Communication." Give the groups 5 minutes to work.

2. Invite each group to present its newsprint sheet to the other groups, and to post the sheet on a wall when they are done. When all the sheets are posted, ask the following questions:
- What do you see repeated in the groups' commandments?
- Is there anything missing? If so, what?

3. Conclude the activity by encouraging the participants to practice good communication skills in the weeks and months ahead. Offer these suggestions for success:
- Follow the commandments listed by the groups. [Name a few that got a lot of attention.]
- Be good listeners by giving others your attention and sending feedback to let them know that you are hearing and understanding them.
- Try to avoid using roadblocks during conversations.

TryThis

Post the "Ten Commandments of Communication" lists in a community meeting room to remind the young people about good communication skills. Or combine the efforts of the groups, and create and post one set of commandments.

Pray It

Listening to God (5 minutes)

Preparation

- Gather the following items:
  - ❏ a *Catholic Youth Bible* or other Bible
  - ❏ a candle and matches
  - ❏ a small table or a cloth
  - ❏ a copy of resource 4, "Listening to God," cut apart as scored
  - ❏ copies of *Spirit & Song* or another hymnal, one for each participant
- Arrange a prayer space in one of two ways: place the Bible and the candle on a small table, or place a cloth on the floor and arrange the Bible and the candle on it.
- Ask for ten volunteers to help with prayer. Give each volunteer one of the Scripture passages from resource 4. Note that the readings are numbered and should be read in order. Ask the recruits each to pause 30 seconds after the preceding person has read before beginning their reading. Be sure each volunteer knows who is reading before him or her.

   1. Invite the participants to sit in a circle around the prayer focus. Begin the prayer by making the sign of the cross and lighting the candle.

   2. Offer the following opening prayer:

- Gracious and loving God, you have called us into relationship with you through your words, your touch, your presence in our lives. We pause today to simply and quietly listen, and to pray to you through our own words, spoken in private.

   3. Invite the readers to proclaim their Scripture passages in order, with a 30-second pause for silent prayer after each passage.

   4. Offer the following closing prayer:

- Lord, help us listen to you more carefully in our lives. May we hear you in the rustle of the leaves and the songs of the birds. May we hear you in the voices of our friends and in the cries of a newborn baby. May we hear you in the silence of our hearts and in the joy of communal celebration. Help us, Lord, to answer your call as Samuel did: "Speak, Lord, for your servant is listening" (1 Sam. 3:9).

   5. End with a selection from the *Spirit & Song* Connections in this chapter, or with a song of your own choosing.

A Picture Says
a Thousand Words

A Communication Process

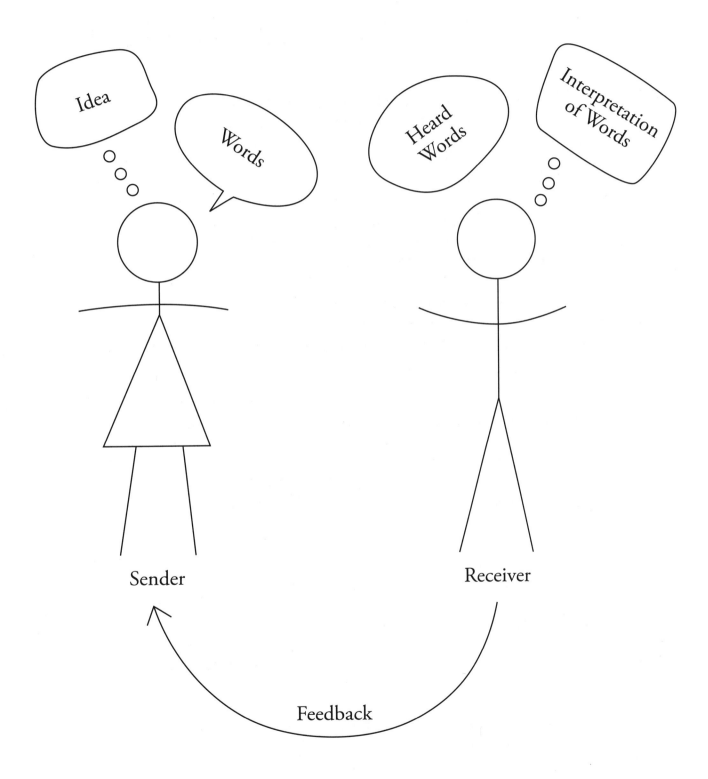

Roadblocks to Effective Communication

Some discussion methods tend to intensify problems rather than alleviate them. Those are called roadblocks to effective communication. Twelve roadblocks are as follows.

Judging

1. Judging, criticizing, blaming: "That's really immature."

2. Name-calling, ridiculing: "You're such a baby!"

3. Interpreting, diagnosing: "You're just jealous of her."

4. Praising, agreeing: "Well, I think you're pretty (or smart or a great player)."

Sending Solutions

5. Ordering, directing, commanding: "Don't ever talk to me like that!"

6. Warning, admonishing, threatening: "If you do that, you'll be sorry."

7. Exhorting, moralizing, preaching: "You ought to do this: . . ."

Avoiding the Other's Concerns

8. Advising or giving solutions: "Just go make friends with someone else."

9. Diverting, distracting: "Why don't you try burning down the school?"

10. Lecturing, teaching, giving logical arguments: "Let's look at the facts: . . ."

11. Reassuring, sympathizing: "Don't worry, everything will work out fine."

(The material on this resource is adapted from *People Skills: How to Assert Yourself, Listen to Others, and Resolve Conflicts,* by Robert Bolton [New York: Simon and Schuster, 1979], pages 17–26. Copyright © 1979 by Simon and Schuster. Adapted with permission of Simon and Schuster Adult Publishing Group.)

Listening to God

✂

1

The Lord God has given me
> the tongue of a teacher,
that I may know how to sustain
> the weary with a word.
Morning by morning he wakens—
> wakens my ear
> to listen as those who are taught.
The Lord God has opened my ear,
> and I was not rebellious,
> I did not turn backward.

(Isaiah 50:4–5, NRSV)

2

Listen carefully to me . . .
Incline your ear, and come to me;
> listen, so that you may live.

(Isaiah 55:2–3, NRSV)

3

In distress you called, and I rescued you;
> I answered you in the secret place of thunder;
> I tested you at the waters of Meribah.

Hear, O my people, while I admonish you;
> O Israel, if you would but listen to me!

(Psalm 81:7–8, NRSV)

4

After three days they found him in the temple, sitting among
the teachers, listening to them and asking them questions.
(Luke 2:46, NRSV)

5

One does not live by bread alone,
> but by every word that comes from the mouth of God.

(Matthew 4:4, NRSV)

6

The reason I speak to them in parables is that "seeing they do not perceive, and hearing they do not listen, nor do they understand." With them indeed is fulfilled the prophecy of Isaiah that says:
You will indeed listen, but never understand,
  and you will indeed look, but never perceive.
For this people's heart has grown dull,
  and their ears are hard of hearing
    and they have shut their eyes;
    so that they might not look with their eyes,
  and listen with their ears.
  and understand with their heart and turn—
    and I would heal them.

(Matthew 13:13–16, NRSV)

7

Now the Lord came and stood there, calling as before, "Samuel! Samuel!" And Samuel said, "Speak, for your servant is listening." (1 Samuel 3:10, NRSV)

8

Whoever listens to you listens to me, and whoever rejects you rejects me, and whoever rejects me rejects the one who sent me. (Luke 10:16, NRSV)

9

You must understand this, my beloved: let everyone be quick to listen, slow to speak. (James 1:19, NRSV)

10

In the beginning was the Word, and the Word was with God, and the Word was God. (John 1:1, NRSV)

11 Leading Group Discussions

Pray It

◆ We Thank God
  for Role Models
  (5 minutes)

Study It

Core Session:
Leading Group Discussions
(60 minutes)

◆ Learning from Others
  (10 minutes)

◆ Tips for Successful
  Facilitation
  (20 minutes)

◆ Practicing Facilitation
  Skills
  (30 minutes)

Overview

As leaders, the young people will be asked to facilitate a variety of groups. This session helps them develop the skills they will need to successfully lead groups and allows them to practice leading a small-group discussion.

Outcomes

◆ The participants will learn how to effectively lead group discussions.
◆ The participants will practice facilitation skills.

Background Reading

◆ Scriptural connections: 2 Chron. 1:7–10 (Solomon's prayer for wisdom), 1 Thess. 1:2–6 (faith and example), Titus 2:7–8 (Paul's advice to Titus)
◆ *Catholic Youth Bible* article connections: "God, Give Me Wisdom" (1 Kings 3:4–15), "Be Not Afraid" (Isa. 43:1–5), "Fill Me, Lord" (Gal. 5:22–26)

We Thank God for Role Models (5 minutes)

Preparation

Spirit & Song connections

◆ "One Spirit, One Church," by Kevin Keil
◆ "Send Out Your Spirit," by Jesse Manibusan

❑ Gather copies of *Spirit & Song* or another hymnal, one for each participant.

❑ Select a closing song from the *Spirit & Song* Connections for this chapter, or another song that fits the theme.

1. Invite the participants to sit in a circle. Make the sign of the cross, and then read the following opening prayer:

- Loving God, throughout history you have called great men and women into leadership. Today you call us. Open our hearts and our minds so that our time together may further prepare for us for our ministry. Teach us, through the example of your Son, Jesus, and the examples of great leaders from our lives, how to become better at leading discussions. Fill us with your spirit of service so that we might empty ourselves of preoccupations and learn to be fully present to those we are called to lead. We ask this through Jesus, our example. Amen.

2. Say:

- In the spirit of prayer, we thank God for the people who have been placed in our lives to teach us about leadership just by the way they live. At this time, I invite you to quietly think about and then pray for a leader (perhaps a teacher, a youth minister, a parent, a friend, or anyone else) who is really skilled at helping groups have good discussions.

Allow a minute of silence.

3. Tell the participants that you are going to ask them to say aloud the names of the leaders they brought to mind. Begin the offering of names by praying:

- Loving God, we thank you for the leaders who model for us how to serve others. Today we especially thank you for . . . [Invite the participants to share the names of the leaders they brought to mind.]

4. Conclude by saying:

- For these and all great leaders who teach us about serving others, we offer thanks by praying the Lord's Prayer.

Lead the group in the Lord's Prayer, followed by the closing song you selected.

Core Session:
Leading Group Discussions (60 minutes)

Preparation

• Gather the following items:
- ❑ pens or pencils
- ❑ sheets of blank paper, one for each participant
- ❑ newsprint and markers
- ❑ copies of resource 5, "Discussion Role-Plays," one for every group of six participants
- ❑ blank envelopes, one for every six to eight participants
- ❑ copies of handout 18, "Learning from the Discussion Role-Plays," two for every six to eight participants

• You will need one scenario from resource 5 for every small group of six to eight participants. If you have more than four groups, you may give multiple groups copies of the same scenario. Cut the copies of the resource apart as scored. For each scenario, tape the discussion topic to the front of an envelope, or, if you choose a topic that is not listed on the resource, write it on the envelope. Then place the eight participant roles in the envelope. If some groups will have fewer than eight participants, pull out enough of the "yourself" roles to make the number of roles equal to the number of participants in the group.

Learning from Others (10 minutes)

1. Ask the participants each to find a partner. Say:

• Think about the leader you prayed for, and the things he or she did to facilitate a good discussion. Then share with your partner what the leader did to encourage group discussion.

Give the participants 5 minutes to discuss. While the sharing is taking place, hand a pen or a pencil to each participant and a sheet of blank paper to each pair.

2. Ask the pairs to list the strategies for leading good discussions that they discussed. Allow 3 minutes for this task.

Tips for Successful Facilitation (20 minutes)

1. Explain to the participants the following instructions:

- I will ask the pair on my right to share the first idea that is listed on its sheet of paper. I will record that answer on newsprint. If the same idea (or something close to it) is on the list you and your partner created, cross it out.
- When it is your pair's turn, please share only an idea not already listed on the newsprint. If you have nothing left on your page, simply tell me to move on to the next pair.

Begin the process by asking the first pair on your right:

- What is one helpful thing the leaders you prayed for did to get people to participate in a group discussion?"

2. Move through all the pairs, using the process explained in step 1. Once the participants have exhausted their answers, it might be necessary to provide some additional insights into group facilitation. If the following ideas have not been mentioned, add them to the newsprint:

- A good facilitator
  - allows each person the opportunity to speak or to remain silent when questions are presented
  - gives each individual the opportunity to not discuss if she or he feels uncomfortable sharing
  - is respectful, honest, and open
  - uses good eye contact
  - listens attentively and responds when appropriate
  - uses humor when appropriate
  - makes sure everyone has the opportunity to share once before someone shares a second time
  - respects silence

3. Ask the participants to silently review the list and choose what they believe are the five most important tips to keep in mind.

4. Invite the participants to come forward a few at a time to the newsprint and place a check mark in front of each of the five ideas they believe are most important.

5. Choose the top ten tips by circling the responses on the newsprint that received the most check marks.

Practicing Facilitation Skills (30 minutes)

1. Form small groups of six to eight participants. Give each group one of the role-play scenario envelopes that you prepared from resource 5. Tell the groups not to open the envelopes until you have completed your instructions.

TryThis

- List the top ten ideas on a fresh sheet of newsprint, and post them in a public place whenever small groups will be discussing.
- While the session continues, have a leader list the top ten ideas on 8½-by-11-inch paper and make enough copies for all the participants. At the end of the session, distribute the copies.

2. Explain the role-plays by saying:

- Each small group has received an envelope describing a role-play scenario.
- Each person in the group will have a role to play in the group's scenario. Inside the envelope are slips of paper describing the roles. One person will take the role of leader, and that person's job will be to try to lead a good group discussion, using all the ideas that we have previously discussed.
- All the other group members are to play their roles as described on the slips that they receive. Once we begin, it is important that everyone play their parts.
- You will have 10 minutes for your discussion.
- Are there any questions? [Address any questions.]
- Begin your role-plays by reading the description on the outside of the envelope and distributing the roles from inside the envelope. Every person in the group should receive a role. Do not tell your group the role you have received.

3. After 10 minutes, stop the role-plays. Invite the groups to reflect on the experience. Give each group a copy of handout 18, and ask the participants to talk through each question within their group. Tell them they have about 5 minutes to discuss.

4. Have each group return its scenario and roles to the envelope. Then have the groups exchange envelopes. Tell them to read the description on the envelope and to distribute the new roles to the group members. Allow 10 minutes for the second round of role-plays.

5. Ask the groups to again use handout 18 to talk about their experience.

6. Invite the participants to share with the large group their responses to this question:

- What are the key points you want to remember about group facilitation? Make comments like the ones that follow if the participants do not offer them:
- As a facilitator, your role is to focus on the group's interactions more than it is to give your perspective on the topic being discussed.
- As a facilitator, you have tremendous influence over the group. Modeling appropriate behavior, as we discussed during the session, will help create a safe environment for the participants.
- As a facilitator, your role is to ensure that everyone has the opportunity to share their thoughts during the discussion. Everyone should be given the opportunity to participate, even those who may wish to pass.

TryThis

- ◆ Invite the participants to learn more about leading discussions by watching how others facilitate discussions in their schools, in their homes, on television, in youth ministry, in the parish, where they work, and in other places.
- ◆ Invite the young people to use the skills learned in this session when they and their friends are trying to figure out what to do on Saturday night, when they are talking about an important issue, or any time they are engaged in a group discussion.

Familyconnections

Invite the participants to ask their parents to tell them about people who they believe are great at enlivening discussions and leading others to share.

Discussion Role-Plays

Seven discussion topics are suggested on this resource: four are listed with participant roles in complete scenarios, and three more are listed separately at the end of the resource. Choose the topics you think will generate good discussion within a small group of your participants. You can replace any of the topics on this resource with ones that you think will be more timely or interesting to your participants. Make sure the topics you choose are likely to invite differences of opinion.

Scenario 1

Discussion topic. Should high school uniforms be mandatory?

Leader. Let the group know you are the leader. Guide the group through the discussion, incorporating the facilitating tips we just discussed.

Observer. Participate in the discussion, but focus on how the leader is facilitating it. You will be asked to give the leader and the group feedback at the end of the role-play. Do not disclose your role until the end of the role-play.

Yourself. Participate in the discussion as you would normally.

Yourself. Participate in the discussion as you would normally.

Yourself. Participate in the discussion as you would normally.

Yourself. Participate in the discussion as you would normally.

Very quiet participant. Do not speak unless you are invited to do so by the leader.

Very passionate participant. Speak as frequently as you can, to try to convince others of your point of view. Follow any directions the leader gives you.

Scenario 2

Discussion topic. Should dances sponsored by Catholic schools or parishes ban music that does not promote Catholic values?

Leader. Let the group know you are the leader. Guide the group through the discussion, incorporating the facilitating tips we just discussed.

Observer. Participate in the discussion, but focus on how the leader is facilitating it. You will be asked to give the leader and the group feedback at the end of the role-play. Do not disclose your role until the end of the role-play.

Yourself. Participate in the discussion as you would normally.

Yourself. Participate in the discussion as you would normally.

Yourself. Participate in the discussion as you would normally.

Yourself. Participate in the discussion as you would normally.

Angry participant. Express your point of view with anger. Follow any directions the leader gives you.

Uninterested participant. Show your lack of interest in the topic through your body language. Follow any directions the leader gives you.

Scenario 3

Discussion topic. What can the Church do to attract young people to Mass?

Leader. Let the group know you are the leader. Guide the group through the discussion, incorporating the facilitating tips we just discussed.

Observer. Participate in the discussion, but focus on how the leader is facilitating it. You will be asked to give the leader and the group feedback at the end of the role-play. Do not disclose your role until the end of the role-play.

Yourself. Participate in the discussion as you would normally.

Yourself. Participate in the discussion as you would normally.

Yourself. Participate in the discussion as you would normally.

Yourself. Participate in the discussion as you would normally.

Very quiet participant. Do not speak unless you are invited to do so by the leader.

Uninterested participant. Show your lack of interest in the topic through your body language. Follow any directions the leader gives you.

Scenario 4

Discussion topic. Why are reality television shows popular?

Leader. Let the group know you are the leader. Guide the group through the discussion, incorporating the facilitating tips we just discussed.

Observer. Participate in the discussion, but focus on how the leader is facilitating it. You will be asked to give the leader and the group feedback at the end of the role-play. Do not disclose your role until the end of the role-play.

Yourself. Participate in the discussion as you would normally.

Yourself. Participate in the discussion as you would normally.

Yourself. Participate in the discussion as you would normally.

Always-talking participant. Speak your mind as often as you can. Follow any directions the leader gives you.

Argumentative participant. As often as you can, counter what people are saying by arguing the other point of view. Follow any directions the leader gives you.

Uninterested participant. Show your lack of interest in the topic through your body language. Follow any directions the leader gives you.

Other Discussion Topics

Discussion topic. Should pirating music over the Internet be legalized?

Discussion topic. Who is the best music artist of all time?

Discussion topic. Should all states prohibit capital punishment?

Learning from the Discussion Role-Plays

Designate someone to lead the group through these discussion questions.

- Ask the role-play leader these questions:
  - How do you think you did leading the group?
  - What made leading the group difficult?
  - Which of the ideas about leading group discussions that we talked about earlier did you try to use?

- Ask the rest of the small-group participants to give the role-play leader feedback by answering the following questions:
  - What did the leader do well?
  - What tips can you give that person for future use?

- Ask all the role-play participants this question:
  - What did you learn from this role-play about leading a group?

- Ask the role-play observer these questions:
  - What did you observe about the leader?
  - What did you observe about the group?

Negotiating Skills

Overview

As Christian leaders, we strive to find solutions that meet the needs of all parties involved in conflict. This session gives the participants an opportunity to learn about and practice win-win interactions to develop better negotiating skills.

An important part of win-win interactions is listening effectively. Consider using chapters 15 and 16, the "Attentive Listening Skills" and "Reflective Listening Skills" minisessions, in this manual before conducting this session if you have not already introduced the participants to those skills.

Outcomes

◆ The participants will learn the necessary skills to handle conflict.
◆ The participants will practice win-win negotiation.

Background Reading

◆ Scriptural connections: Matt. 5:23–24 (Be reconciled with one another.), Matt. 5:43–48 (Love your enemies.), Matt. 18:15–19 (Reprove those who sin against you.)
◆ *Catholic Youth Bible* article connections: "A Prayer for Understanding" (Josh. 22:13–20), "Courage" (Psalm 31), "Count to Ten" (Prov. 17:14)

AT A GLANCE

Pray It

◆ A Prayer from Saint Francis
(5 minutes)

Study It

Core Session: Negotiating Skills
(55 minutes)

◆ Does Win-Win Exist in the Real World?
(20 minutes)

◆ Win-Win Negotiation
(15 minutes)

◆ Practicing Win-Win Negotiation
(20 minutes)

Session Extension

◆ In-Depth Role-Plays to Practice Win-Win Interactions
(30 minutes)

Spirit & Song connections

- "Go Make a Difference," by Steve Angrisano and Tom Tomaszek
- "Lead Me, Lord," by John D. Becker
- "Prayer of St. Francis," by Sebastian Temple

Pray It

A Prayer from Saint Francis (5 minutes)

Preparation

- Gather the following items:
  - ❑ copies of handout 19, "The Peace Prayer Attributed to Saint Francis of Assisi," one for each participant
  - ❑ a *Catholic Youth Bible* or other Bible, marked at Matt. 5:38–48
- Invite a participant to proclaim the Scripture reading.

1. Distribute handout 19. Then call the participants into a moment of silence to center themselves and to remember that they live in the presence of a peaceful, loving God.

2. Invite the volunteer to proclaim Matt. 5:38–48. Allow a moment of quiet reflection.

3. Ask the participants to pray aloud together the prayer attributed to Saint Francis of Assisi from the handout.

4. Encourage the participants to give one another a sign of peace.

Core Session:
Negotiating Skills (55 minutes)

Preparation

- Gather the following items:
  - ❏ newsprint
  - ❏ markers
  - ❏ copies of handout 20, "Ways of Interacting," one for every six to eight participants
  - ❏ pens or pencils
  - ❏ copies of handout 21, "Steps to a Win-Win Solution," one for each participant
- Enlarge the diagram from handout 20 on a sheet of newsprint or an overhead projection.

Does Win-Win Exist in the Real World? (20 minutes)

1. Introduce the session by saying:

- Our time together for this session will focus on building negotiating skills. We'll be working through some problems by thinking about and practicing win-win negotiation.

2. Using the comments that follow and referring to the enlargement of the diagram from handout 20, introduce the idea of win-win negotiating. As you explain each way of interacting, write an example of it in the corresponding quadrant on the diagram.

- We use four basic ways of interacting when we negotiate.
- In lose-lose, both parties lose. For example, lose-lose occurs when a child stops playing soccer and takes his ball home. He is no longer playing (lose), and his friends cannot play either (lose).
- Win-lose occurs when one person wins at the expense of another person. For example, if you always want or get your way, you believe that getting along, building relationships, and sharing with others are secondary to being the best or having things a certain way.
- Lose-win occurs when one person allows another to win at his or her own expense. For example, if you allow someone to persuade you to do something you would not normally do because it is against your values or principles, you end up in a lose-win situation.

- Finally, win-win allows both parties to win. For example, if you donate gently used clothing to the Saint Vincent de Paul Society, you win because you live more simply, and poor people in the community win because they have clothes to wear.
- Let us begin our discussion on negotiating skills by reflecting on those four ways in which we interact.

3. Form small groups of six to eight participants. Distribute handout 20, and pens or pencils. Issue the following instructions:
- Designate someone in the group to serve as the recorder.
- Each group should create a list of examples of each type of interaction. The recorder should place the examples in the appropriate quadrants as I did on my copy of the diagram. For instance, under "Win-lose," you might want to give the example of one sports team beating another sports team. You may begin.

4. After 5 minutes, instruct the participants to stop listing. Have each group count how many different interactions it could name. Solicit responses and declare the winner (the one with the most responses).

5. Invite the winning group to name all the interactions it listed in each quadrant. Then solicit more examples of win-win from the other groups.

6. Ask the participants:
- How could this activity have been a win-win activity for all involved?
Invite a few responses. Give the following examples if they are not shared:
- by giving each group a different quadrant on which to work, thus eliminating any sense of competition
- by not declaring a winner
- by inviting all the groups to share their examples

7. Conclude this part of the session by saying:
- There is a time and a place to use each way of interacting. Competition is sometimes a good motivator. Unfortunately in our society it is often the only motivator people know. What we are trying to learn today is a way of interacting that moves away from winners and losers and finds viable solutions where all parties can win.

Win-Win Negotiation (15 minutes)

1. Ask the participants this question:
- What do you find most challenging about trying to achieve win-win solutions?
Note the participants' responses on newsprint.

2. Add these comments to the discussion:

- Our culture usually shows us lose-win, win-lose, or lose-lose interaction. Think about reality TV shows—they are all about lose-lose, lose-win, or win-lose. We rarely see all winners.
- A win-win solution can be difficult to achieve. People need to be committed to working on a solution that meets everyone's needs.
- It is easier to exert power over someone like bullies do. Yet true leadership is sharing power by seeking win-win solutions.
- Many times we find ourselves in an environment that does not foster trust. If you try to come up with a win-win solution, people often think you are trying to take advantage of them.

3. Integrate the Gospel message from Matt. 5:38–48 into this discussion by including points such as these:

- Jesus was always trying to find win-win solutions. He was always trying to find ways to be inclusive and to meet people's needs. He hung around the people whose needs were always excluded, and he challenged those who used their power to intimidate others. Jesus invited prostitutes, outcasts, and tax collectors to dine with him.
- Jesus sat with the woman at the well—an outcast—and listened to her story and found a way to use her gifts for the community. That was a win-win situation—a win for the Samaritan woman because she did not think she had any gifts to share, and a win for her community because through her they heard about Jesus.
- James and John asked Jesus, "Grant us to sit, one at your right hand and one at your left, in your glory" (Mark 10:37)—clearly a win-lose proposition. Jesus turned it around and asked, "Are you able to drink the cup that I drink?" (v. 38). He was asking, "Who is willing to try to find win-win solutions for our society, solutions where everyone is treated equally?"
- Jesus gives us clear examples of the key win-win negotiating steps. Let us look at those steps in detail.

4. Distribute handout 21. Review the handout, and explain the steps by saying:

- Step 1 is probably the most challenging part of win-win. We must listen by emptying ourselves and being open to hearing other people's needs and issues. Win-win is about letting down our defenses and listening with our hearts, our minds, our emotions, and our whole selves. We must listen until we experience the other people's perspectives and truly understand. In this step, we reflect what the other people are saying until they feel heard.
- In step 2 those involved must let go of the solutions or specific positions they have in mind and be open to other possibilities. Here we name the needs, issues, and concerns of both parties. In the first step, we tried to be

open to the other parties' needs, and in this step we also need to be able to clearly state our own needs. The temptation is to name the specific solution we have in mind. The challenge is to separate the needs from solutions.

- Step 3 determines what results will constitute a fully acceptable solution. In this step, we name what is needed for a viable solution. The key question to ask is, "What would win-win look like?"
- In step 4 we identify possible options to achieve the desired results. This is the fun part. Here we can come up with as many crazy solutions as we want because the idea is to brainstorm solutions. We have lots of creative freedom. After brainstorming, we evaluate using the criteria from step 3. We eliminate the solutions that do not fit the criteria, and end up with a solution that works for everyone.

5. Explain the challenges of working toward win-win negotiation with others, as follows:

- It sounds easy enough, but win-win negotiation is hard work. Not everyone will want to put in the time and effort needed to achieve a win-win solution.
- Not everyone listens to another point of view. When we enter conflict, we often stop listening and dig in our heels.
- Often we see only one solution (ours!) and enter a dialogue thinking that unless we get the solution we want, nothing else counts.
- We can become defensive, angry, or judgmental. When we think negotiation is all about defending why we want this solution and why no other solution is acceptable, achieving win-win is difficult or impossible.

Practicing Win-Win Negotiation (20 minutes)

1. Invite the participants to help you solve the following issue:

- The issue is a typical family conflict. This family has two teenagers who can both drive. Monica needs to get to work by 4:30 p.m., and Daniel needs to stay at school for volleyball practice until 5:30 p.m. Public transportation is not available in their town, and only one car is available to them. They are fighting about who should get the car. Both Monica and Daniel have brought strong cases to their parents. Their parents, who have just heard about win-win negotiation, are trying it out to solve this issue.

2. Walk with the participants through the four steps of win-win negotiation and help them determine a potential solution. A few options for each step are listed here.

- *Step 1.* The family identifies the following perspectives:
  - Getting to work on time is really important to Monica because she just started a new job and she wants to make a good first impression.

TryThis

Select an example such as a conflict between friends, a family issue, a youth ministry or parish concern, or a school-related problem. Use that example as an alternative to the one provided in step 1 of this activity, and proceed through the process outlined in step 2.

- Daniel really likes playing volleyball, and he is afraid of being cut from the team because the coach has a policy that says players cannot miss more than three practices.

- *Step 2.* The family identifies these key issues and concerns:
  - Monica needs to get to work by 4:30 p.m. at the latest.
  - Daniel needs to stay for all volleyball practices.
  - Monica needs to arrive on time because she just started her job.

  Note that the car is not mentioned as a need. Who has use of the car is a solution—it is not a need. Only the needs are listed.

- *Step 3.* The family identifies the following results as together constituting a fully acceptable solution:
  - Monica arrives to work by 4:30 p.m. at the latest.
  - Daniel stays for volleyball practice.

  Note that the car is a "nice-to-have" and not a "must-have." The two results listed here are "must-haves."

- *Step 4.* The family identifies several possible new options for achieving the required results:
  - Daniel gets a ride with a teammate the nights that Monica works.
  - Monica takes a cab to work, and Monica and Daniel split the cost. Daniel picks her up at the end of her shift.
  - Daniel rides his bike to school the days Monica has to work, and then rides it back home after volleyball practice.
  - Daniel asks his coach if he can leave at about 4:15 p.m. to drive his sister to work. This will take him out of practice for 20 minutes. Daniel then picks up Monica after work.
  - Monica buys a new car with her money!

  Note that this is a brainstormed list, and all ideas are written down. The family then uses the criteria stated in step 3 to evaluate each idea. An acceptable solution is identified and given a trial period before the family evaluates whether the solution is effective.

3. Close the session by asking the participants:

- What do you think is most challenging about win-win interactions?

Share the following thoughts if they are not offered by the participants:

- Win-win interactions are a concrete way of living out the Gospel message. Although it takes time, effort, and energy, win-win negotiation seeks first to understand. It ensures that everyone's needs are met and focuses on power *with* each other instead of power over another.

- Thinking and acting in a win-win fashion is challenging. I encourage you to make an effort to integrate this into your everyday life; you will be amazed at the positive results that can occur.

TryThis

To make the example more realistic, invite two participants to assume the roles of the teenagers. Ask another two participants to be the parents. Ask the actors to work through the negotiating steps as a role-play in front of the rest of the group. As the role-play unfolds, invite participants in the group to give input. This alternative will add about 10 minutes to the session.

TryThis

Challenge the participants to use win-win negotiations in their everyday life. Invite them to begin by focusing on listening to the other point of view before defending their own. Give them simple phrases such as these to use to help them focus on coming up with win-win solutions:

◆ What I hear you saying is . . .

◆ What do you need?

◆ What about if we try . . .

Familyconnections

◆ Conduct a workshop for parents on win-win negotiations. If you think the young people are ready, invite them to facilitate the workshop for their parents.

◆ Invite the young people to use their new skills in the next conflict that arises at home.

Mediaconnections

◆ *Ghandi* (Columbia Pictures, 190 minutes, 1982, rated PG). This movie highlights Gandhi's stance on negotiating with those in power.

Session Extension

In-Depth Role-Plays to Practice Win-Win Interactions (30 minutes)

Preparation

• Gather the following items:

❑ copies of resource 6, "Win-Win Role-Plays," one for every twenty to twenty-four participants

❑ copies of handout 22, "Assessing the Role-Plays," one for every five or six participants

• Find a meeting space that will allow each small group of five or six participants enough room to work through its role-play.

• You will need one role-play from resource 6 for every small group of five or six participants. If you have more than four small groups, you may give multiple groups copies of the same role-plays. Cut apart the copies of the resource as scored.

1. Form small groups of five or six participants. Distribute one role-play scenario from resource 6 to each group. Have participants refer to handout 21, which they received in the previous session, and give each group a copy of handout 22.

2. Explain the win-win role-plays by saying this:

• We are now going to practice win-win interactions through role-plays.

• Each small group has been given a scenario for which it needs to find a win-win solution.

• In each scenario, one person—or two people if your group has six people—will be an observer. The observer watches the interactions and gives feedback at the end, using the handout provided. The observer is also the timekeeper.

• Each group has 20 minutes for its scenario: 5 minutes to prepare, 10 minutes to role-play, and 5 minutes to receive feedback from the observer.

3. Assign each small group an area where it can perform the role-play. Invite the participants to begin. Circulate through the small groups to answer any questions.

4. After 20 minutes, regather the participants into a large group. Solicit comments about their role-play experience by asking the following questions:

• What did you find most challenging about win-win interactions?

• What went well?

• What do you want to remember?

The Peace Prayer Attributed to Saint Francis of Assisi

Lord, make me an instrument of your peace,
Where there is hatred, let me sow love.
Where there is injury, pardon.
Where there is doubt, faith.
Where there is despair, hope.
Where there is darkness, light.
Where there is sadness, joy.

O Divine Master, grant that I may not so much seek
To be consoled as to console,
to be understood as to understand,
to be loved as to love.
For it is in giving that we receive.
It is in pardoning that we are pardoned.
And it is in dying that we are born to eternal life.

(The prayer on this handout is from *Six Ways to Pray from Six Great Saints,* by Gloria Hutchinson [Cincinnati: Saint Anthony Messenger Press, 1982], page 24. Copyright © 1982 by Saint Anthony Messenger Press.)

Ways of Interacting

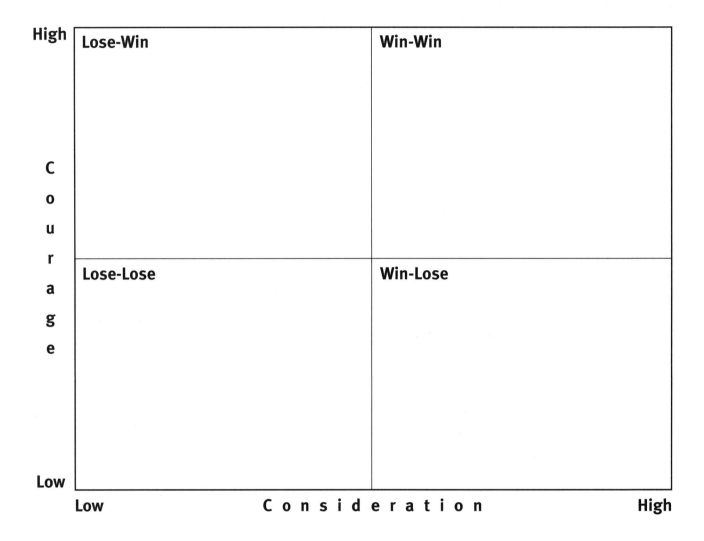

Steps to a Win-Win Solution

Step 1: Listen to the other person and see the problem from his or her perspective.

Hints

- Put yourself in the other's shoes—seek to understand.
- Give expression to the needs and the concerns of the other.
- Listen attentively and reflect what the other is saying.
- Empty yourself of your agenda and defenses.

Step 2: Identify the needs (key issues and concerns—not positions) of all involved.

Hints

- Make a list of all the needs—issues and concerns.
- Move away from positions.
- Be concrete. Ask why? or why not?
- Be flexible.

Step 3: Determine what results would constitute a fully acceptable solution.

Hints

- Make a list.
- Focus on "must-haves" versus "nice-to-haves," such as *I must* get to work on time versus *it would be nice* to have the car to get there.

Step 4: Identify possible new options to achieve those results.

Hints

- Brainstorm as many solutions as possible. Do not evaluate any idea, even if it seems unattainable.
- Think outside the box.
- Evaluate the brainstormed ideas based on the criteria arrived at in step 3.
- Consider which of these solutions meet the needs of all parties.

Win-Win Role-Plays

Scenario 1

For years your school has contemplated having uniforms. The principal and vice-principals, along with the parent council, have agreed that uniforms will be implemented in the next school year. The students are upset that this decision has been made without their input. Many are against wearing uniforms because doing so would limit their ability to express their individuality. The student council has requested a meeting with the principal and the parent council to discuss this situation.

Roles

a student council, a principal, a parent council, an observer

Scenario 2

Your parish has offered a Sunday evening coffeehouse for senior youth for the past year. It is an informal event where young people can drop in, chat, and listen to music. It has been received well by the young people. The coordinating team provides some music, but the young people are also welcome to bring music that does not contain offensive language. Recently, because of complaints from parishioners, the pastor and parish council have informed the coordinating team that only liturgical music can be played during the coffeehouse. The parishioners who made the complaint think that it is not appropriate to play other music in the church—a sacred space—and believe that the music the youth were playing did not promote Christian values. The coordinating team believes that the new rule will decrease the number of young people who attend and change the atmosphere of the evening. They have requested a meeting with the pastor and the parish council chair.

Roles

a coordinating team, a pastor, a parish council chair, an observer

Scenario 3

For months a group of your close friends has been planning to attend a New Year's Eve party about forty-five minutes north of your community. Recently a group of teenagers were killed on the highway north of the community while returning from a weekend getaway. Your concerned parents have talked it over and decided they are not allowing their teens to attend the party. You and your friends are very disappointed. As a group, you have requested a formal meeting with all your parents to discuss this matter.

Roles

a group of friends, a group of parents, an observer

Scenario 4

Recently at lunch at your school, a fight broke out between two guys over one of your girlfriends. The supervising teacher, knowing that you and a friend were taking this training session, has asked both of you to use the win-win process in mediation to help the guys solve their differences. Your role is to help the guys go through the win-win steps and come up with a solution they can both live with.

Roles

two guys, two mediators, one or more observers

Assessing the Role-Plays

Observer's Checklist

Use this checklist to observe the role-play and give the group feedback.

1. How well did the group work through each of the win-win steps?
   ❏ **Step 1:** Listen to the other person and see the problem from his or her perspective.

   ❏ **Step 2:** Identify the needs of all involved.

   ❏ **Step 3:** Determine what results would constitute a fully acceptable solution.

   ❏ **Step 4:** Identify possible new options to achieve those results.

2. Did they find a win-win solution?

3. What went well?

4. What needs improvement?

AT A GLANCE

Study It

Core Session:
Planning Skills
(55 minutes)

- Planning a Vacation
  (15 minutes)
- Small-Group Discussion
  (10 minutes)
- Principles of Planning
  (10 minutes)
- Practicing Planning Skills
  (20 minutes)

Pray It

- Keeping Jesus
  at the Center
  (10 minutes)

13 Planning Skills

Overview

Many young people are asked to plan activities and programs. Providing them with opportunities to develop planning skills can increase their confidence in leading and equip them with planning tools for a lifetime. In this session the participants discover effective ways to plan and are able to use their planning skills in a small-group simulation.

Outcomes

- The participants will learn how to plan effectively to achieve good results.
- The participants will practice using planning skills in a simulation.

Background Reading

- Scriptural connections: Prov. 4:25–27 (Keep to the right path.), 2 Cor. 1:17 (Be steadfast in your work.), Col. 3:15–17 (Let Christ rule your life.)
- *Catholic Youth Bible* article connections: "Sharing Responsibility" (Exod. 18:13–26), "Lady Wisdom" (Prov. 8:1–21), "Prepare the Way" (Mal. 3:1–2)

Core Session:
Planning Skills (55 minutes)

Preparation
- Gather the following items:
  - ❑ newsprint and markers
  - ❑ masking tape
  - ❑ copies of handout 23, "Steps for Effective Planning," one for each participant
- On a sheet of newsprint, write the italicized phrases from the bulleted list of instructions in step 2 of the activity "Planning a Vacation."
- On a sheet of newsprint, write the heading "Vacation Discussion" and list the following questions:
  - ❑ What was the first planning step you took?
  - ❑ Who took the lead? How was that person chosen to lead?
  - ❑ Did you name any goals? If so, what were they?
  - ❑ Did you get off track? If so, how did you get back on track?
  - ❑ Did you name others in the community who could help your planning?
  - ❑ In what way was time a factor in your planning?

Planning a Vacation (15 minutes)

    1. Gather the participants and introduce the session by saying:
- An effective leader knows how to plan activities and projects well. Today we will focus on developing our planning skills.

    2. Divide the participants into groups of six to eight. Give the following instructions:
- You are gathered with a group of friends who are *planning a vacation.*
- Your parents have given each of you *$250 to spend on the vacation.*
- Your parents have agreed that *you can go anywhere you like, as long as you all go together.*
- You must provide your parents with a *detailed schedule of your plans.*
- You are planning a *one-week trip.*
- You have 10 minutes to plan.
- Are there any questions? [Address any questions.]

Post your newsprint list of italicized phrases for the groups to refer to as they are planning. Be sure to circulate around to the groups to answer questions and to observe their planning skills.

3. To emphasize the pressure of time on the group, tell the participants when they have 5 minutes remaining. Then tell them when they have 2 minutes and 1 minute. After the activity is completed, the effect of time pressure can be a point to discuss. The groups will not be able to adequately complete the task in the time allotted. Once the steps of planning effectively are discussed, they will have a chance to continue their vacation planning.

Small-Group Discussion (10 minutes)

Post the "Vacation Discussion" questions you prepared on newsprint. Ask the participants to stop, gather into the large group, and reflect on how they planned by discussing those questions. The groups will probably want to share what they have planned. The outcome of their discussion, that is, the details of the vacations, is not what is important. Help the groups focus on the process they used. Suggest that the details of the vacations can be shared at the end of the session, if time allows.

Principles of Planning (10 minutes)

With everyone still in the large group, distribute handout 23. Discuss the main insights on the handout. Use the experience the young people are sharing to connect with the following comments as you work through the handout:

1. Within the planning team, appoint a facilitator (someone who will lead the discussion, keep everyone on track, and move the planning forward), a recorder (someone who will record all decisions that are made), and a timekeeper (someone who will keep track of the time so that it is used effectively).
2. Clearly identify the needs of the group
3. Set distinct goals for the activity, project, or program.
4. Think in terms of partners and resources from outside the group. Who can work with the group? What do you already have and know?
5. Work out the details, including who will do what and by when.
6. Figure out how to ensure the success of the plan.
7. Determine how the activity, project, or program will be evaluated. How will you know if you have reached your goals?

Practicing Planning Skills (20 minutes)

1. Say:

- Now you will have an opportunity to practice those planning principles. Go back to your small group, and continue planning your vacation by using the steps we just discussed.

Give the participants 15 minutes to work in their small groups.

2. Regather the participants and lead a discussion by asking the following questions:

- How helpful were the planning steps in developing your plan?
- What was the most challenging step?
- What could you do to improve your planning skills?

Solicit feedback and respond to their concerns. The participants may express the following ideas, or you may need to add these points to their observations:

- Planning does take time. Setting goals lets everyone know what is expected.
- Identifying resources helps to make the plan doable.
- Building ownership means inviting others to be involved so that they feel a part of the project. A strong sense of ownership within the planning group helps ensure that the plan will not fall apart if a few people opt out.

3. Suggest that the participants use the skills they have just learned in any upcoming planning within their school committees, parish groups, and work situations.

Keeping Jesus at the Center (10 minutes)

Preparation

- Gather the following items:
  - ❏ chairs, one for each participant
  - ❏ a small table
  - ❏ a *Catholic Youth Bible* or other Bible, marked at John 15:1–5
  - ❏ a crucifix
  - ❏ a cloth
  - ❏ a candle and matches
  - ❏ a length of ivy or other vine (optional)
  - ❏ copies of *Spirit & Song* or another hymnal, one for each participant

TryThis

Use chapter 18, the "Effective Meeting Skills" mini-session, as an extension to this session. The participants will have a chance to learn skills for running effective meetings, and those skills can be beneficial for young people who are working together to plan events and programming.

Spirit & Song connections

- ◆ "Behind and Before Me," by Cyprian "Dan" Consiglio
- ◆ "City of God," by Dan Schutte
- ◆ "Find Us Ready," by Tom Booth
- ◆ "What Is Our Service to Be," by Scot Crandal

Familyconnections

Encourage the participants to share this model of planning with their families. The families can use this model for any major planning they are or will be doing.

Mediaconnections

◆ *Apollo 13* (Universal Studios, 1995, 140 minutes, rated PG). This movie includes scenes about the importance of planning, including using only what is available and meeting real needs.

◆ *Field of Dreams* (Universal Studios, 116 minutes, 1989, rated PG). This movie is about planning for the impossible and following your dreams.

• Form a circle with chairs. In the center, place the table with the cloth, the Bible, the crucifix, the candle, and the vine.
• Select a gathering song from the *Spirit & Song* Connections for this chapter, or choose another song that reflects the theme mission.
• Invite a participant to proclaim the Scripture reading.

1. Invite the participants to sit around the prayer table. Distribute hymnals. Light the candle and make the sign of the cross. Spend a moment in silence to move the participants into a prayerful atmosphere. Invite the participants to sing the gathering song you have selected.

2. Pray the opening prayer:
• Faithful God, your Son, Jesus, reminds us that he is the vine and we are the branches. Remind us that as Christian leaders, we must stay deeply connected with you—the source of our strength, inspiration, and hope. We offer our time to you and ask that you link us more closely with your Son that we may produce fruit—fruit that will last.

3. Ask your recruit to proclaim John 15:1–5. Allow time for quiet reflection.

4. Encourage the participants to share with a partner their reflections on the following question:
• What can you do to ensure that you keep Jesus at the center when you plan activities or programs?
Allow 5 minutes for the participants to share their reflections.

5. Regather the participants and lead them in praying the Lord's Prayer.

Steps for Effective Planning

1. Work as a team.

As you plan, who will be the facilitator, the recorder, and the timekeeper?

2. Identify the needs.

What are the needs of the group for whom you are planning?

3. State your goals.

What are you trying to accomplish through this activity, project, or program?

4. Identify partners and resources.

Who in your community can help you meet the goals of your activity, project, or program?

5. Work out the details of your plan.

The plan needs to cover the following key items in detail:

Where?

When?

What is the target audience?

Who will do what?

What is required for each part of the event (for example, prayer, activities, food, speakers)?

6. Create ownership and support.

How will you get the word out about the event? Who will you include to ensure its success?

7. Create an evaluation strategy.

How will you know if your activity, project, or program was a success and what needs to be improved?

Minisessions

14 Large-Group Communication

Overview

When young people are invited to take up-front roles, adults must prepare them and provide them with the needed skills. This minisession helps young people in leadership roles think through the ways they will communicate with others. Use this session as part of a larger leadership training program, or take a few minutes before an event to use it with the young people who have leadership roles in the event.

Outcomes

- The participants will reflect on the elements needed for effective large-group communication.
- The participants will learn skills for making announcements, giving directions, and getting a group's attention.

TryThis

Invite the participants to sign up to help with up-front leadership responsibilities—making announcements, getting the group's attention, leading icebreakers, presiding at prayer, and so on—at future youth ministry events. Provide encouragement and feedback for the young people in those roles, and help them continue to develop their skills.

Core Session: Large-Group Communication (15 minutes)

Preparation
- Gather the following items:
  - ❑ newsprint and markers
  - ❑ copies of handout 24, "When You Are Up Front," one for each participant

What Works and What Doesn't (15 minutes)

1. Welcome the participants, and tell them that today they will learn skills for speaking in front of groups—for giving directions, getting people's attention, and making announcements.

2. Divide a sheet of newsprint down the center. On one side write, "Helpful," and on the other side, write, "Not Helpful." Ask the participants:
- What are some examples of how to get a group's attention or give directions?

Tell the participants that those may be positive or negative examples. Ask them to be clear about what makes the example helpful or not helpful. Note their responses in the appropriate column on the newsprint.

Should you need to offer a few ideas to get the group going, consider these:
- Helpful examples include speaking in a friendly and inviting manner, and using positive words and gestures.
- Unhelpful examples include yelling, blowing a whistle, and banging on a table.

3. Invite discussion using these questions:
- What would your reaction have been if I had started this session by yelling at you to get your attention?
- Why are we more likely to pay attention to someone who uses positive methods of getting our attention?

4. Distribute handout 24. Review the points on the handout with the participants, making connections with what has been noted in the "Helpful" and "Not Helpful" columns on the newsprint.

5. Conclude the session by encouraging the participants to use the skills they have learned in this activity whenever they are in front of a group as a leader, whether at school, in the parish, on the job, or in the community.

When You Are Up Front

Here are some helpful hints to remember when you are the person up front:

- **Know what you want to say.** A group will give you only so much time, so before getting their attention, be sure you know what you want to communicate. It is a good idea to write down what you plan to say. Even if you do not use your notes, you will have something to fall back on, and the exercise of writing will help you prepare.

- **Do not yell.** You might need to use a loud voice to get a group's attention, but project your voice, do not yell. Once you have everyone's attention, speak in an even voice.

- **Do not start speaking until you have the group's attention.** If half the members of the group are not listening, don't start speaking—you will only have to repeat yourself. Ask for attention before you start, and wait until you get everyone's attention before you begin sharing information.

- **When you are going to be leading an activity, make sure you practice giving the directions beforehand.** Giving directions always seems easier to do than it actually is; take the time to practice what you will say so that you can be as clear and concise as possible.

- **Listen to yourself and choose your words carefully.** Often when we get up front, we say things we normally would not (such as, "Shut up!") out of frustration. Find polite ways to ask people to stop talking.

- Any of the following ideas helps groups know when it is time to stop talking.
  - Say, "If you can hear my voice, clap once" (a few people will clap). Then, "If you can hear my voice, clap twice." Then, "If you can hear my voice, clap three times." Usually, by the time you get to three, people are clapping and not talking.
  - Let the group know that when you raise your hand, it is a sign that you would like their attention. They should also raise their hands and stop talking, encouraging those around them to do the same.
  - Develop a phrase that will be a signal to the group that you need their attention. Consider saying, "God is good," and requesting that the group respond by saying, "All the time." Then say, "All the time," and ask the group to respond by saying, "God is good."

15

Attentive Listening Skills

Overview

Good listeners are trusted friends, valued colleagues, and compassionate spouses and parents. This session helps the participants explore the necessary elements of good listening when participating in face-to-face and one-on-one conversations or discussions. The session's simple exercises will have a lasting effect on the participants if they are followed up with encouragement for using good attending skills and with reminders about the lessons they learned.

Outcomes

◆ The participants will experience the effects of poor attending skills.
◆ The participants will recognize the importance of attending skills and will obtain specific information about how to be a good listener.

Core Session: Are You Listening? (40 minutes)

Preparation

- Gather the following items:
  - ❑ newsprint and markers
  - ❑ copies of handout 25, "Attending Skills," one for each participant
- Use a room large enough to hold all the participants in such a way that they can talk in pairs without being too close to one another. The participants will need to sit on the floor during this session.
- Be sure you fully understand all the activity instructions. If possible, practice with a small group before facilitating this session.

Let's Get Talking (30 minutes)

This activity works with any number of people, although the larger the group, the more difficult it might be to facilitate the discussion between rounds. Because you are teaching the importance of good listening skills, getting and keeping attention is essential when facilitating the discussion. Although some reaction (which may be expressed verbally when you call time) is good and natural, make sure the young people begin to practice their listening skills during the discussion.

1. Welcome the participants, and tell them they are going to participate in a series of exercises to teach them more about communication skills. Ask everyone to find a partner, preferably someone they do not know well. Have the partners *stand* facing each other. Instruct the partners to determine who is older. Explain that the older person becomes partner 1 and the younger person becomes partner 2.

2. Give the following instructions for round 1:

- Partner 1, for this round you will be the speaker. Partner 2, you will be the listener.
- Partner 1, your job is to tell all about your family. You must speak for 2 minutes. You can tell about your immediate family, your extended family, your family pet, or whatever. But you must continue speaking until I tell you to stop.

- Partner 2, your job is to listen, and only to listen. You are not allowed to ask questions, tell stories of your own, or say anything. You must simply listen.
- Are there are any questions? [Address any questions.]
- Partner 1, you have one additional instruction. Close your eyes right now and do not open them again until I have called time. [Pause and make sure everyone closes their eyes.] You may begin.

3. While the partner 1s are speaking, quickly and silently remove all the listeners (partner 2s) off to the side of the room, leaving only the speakers in the center of the gathering space. If the crowd is larger than fifteen people, have at least one person help you remove the listening partners. It is best to pause about 20 second after the partners have started talking before removing the listeners, so that the room is noisy. If any speakers open their eyes, quietly tell them to close their eyes and stay where they are.

4. Call time and ask the speakers to open their eyes. Ask the group of partner 1s (those who were speaking):
- How did you feel when you opened your eyes, and why?

Many might tell you *what* they were thinking; press them for feeling words. Make sure you hear from a number of people. Possible answers include, "I was mad," "I was embarrassed," and "I felt like a jerk."

5. Use the following comments and questions to sum up the observations and feelings that have been shared:
- Although we rarely get physically "walked away from" in conversation, we walk away from others in lots of ways when they are talking to us. What are some ways we walk away from others? [Possible answers include, "We doodle," "We get distracted by TV, music, or friends," and "We stop listening and start telling our own stories."]
- Remember that when we walk away from others, they are left feeling angry, embarrassed, and abandoned. [Insert other feelings that the participants mentioned.]

6. Invite the participants to sit on the floor. Give the following instructions for round 2:
- Partner 2, for this round you will be the speaker. Partner 1, you will be the listener.
- Partner 2, your job is to tell your partner all about your family. You must speak for a full minute. You must continue speaking until I tell you to stop.
- Partner 1, your job is to listen, and only to listen. You are not allowed to say anything.
- For this round, you both must maintain constant eye contact. You are not allowed to look away from each other for the entire time.
- Are there any questions? [Address any questions.] You may begin.

7. When 1 minute is up, call time. Ask the partner 2s (those who were speaking):

- How did you feel, and why?

Make sure you hear from many people, because the reactions to eye contact can be very different.

Then ask the partner 1s (those who were listening):

- How was that experience for you, and why?

8. Use the following comments to sum up the observations and feelings that have been shared:

- It is often difficult to maintain good eye contact while speaking face-to face because we often need to look away to gather our thoughts. But for the listener, maintaining eye contact is important.
- This is especially true when a difficult story is being shared. The speaker might not look at the listener often, but wants to know that the listener is still there and is attentive. The speaker will know that if the listener is looking at him or her. Maintaining good eye contact takes work on the part of the listener, but it is an effective tool for communicating interest.
- Different cultures can have different reactions to eye contact, so try to be sensitive when speaking with people outside your own culture. In many Asian and Hispanic cultures, for example, eye contact is a sign of disre-spect, and it would be inappropriate to make eye contact with the person you are speaking to. [If any of your participants come from other cultures, they may be able to share how eye contact is understood in those cultures.]

9. Give the following instructions for round 3:

- Partner 1, for this round you will be the speaker. Partner 2, you will be the listener.
- Partner 1, your job is to tell your partner how to do something physical—like ski, swim, rebuild an engine, or plant a garden. You can choose any-thing you know how to do. Assume that your partner knows nothing about your chosen activity and you have to teach him or her how to do it. You will have 1 minute to talk.
- Partner 2, your job is to listen, and only to listen. You are not allowed to say anything.
- For this round, both partners will sit on their hands.
- Are there any questions? [Address any questions.] You may begin.

10. After 1 minute call time. Ask the partner 1s (those who were speaking):

- Was it difficult, and why?

Make sure you hear from many people. Sum up the observations shared and note some of your own, such as the funny ways you saw the speakers moving or the different ways they used their heads or feet or other body parts to communicate.

Then ask all the participants:
- How much of communication is the words that are spoken?

Allow a number of people to guess. Tell the group that the correct answer (depending on the study) is about 7 percent.

Next ask:
- What do you think makes up the other 93 percent of communication?

Allow for some answers, then offer the following information:
- Research by Albert Mehrabian shows that another 38 percent of communication is tone of voice, and the other 55 percent is body language—what the face, eyes, arms, and rest of the body are doing ("Communication Without Words").

Ask:
- Have you ever broken up with someone over the phone (or worse, through e-mail)? Or have you ever had a fight with a friend over the phone? Why did you not do it in person?

Invite a few answers from the participants, then say:
- Emotions and thoughts get told not only through spoken word, but also through the rest of the body.

11. Give the following instructions for round 4:
- Partner 2, for this round you will be the speaker. Partner 1, you will be the listener.
- Partner 2, your job is to tell your partner about a great day in your life. It doesn't have to be the best day of your life, just a day that you remember fondly.
- Partner 1, your job is to listen as well as you have ever listened—but only with your ears. With every other part of your body, I want you to communicate to your partner that you could care less about what she or he is saying. You cannot physically leave because you need to really listen, but do everything you can to make your partner think you are not listening.
- Are there any questions? [Address any questions.] You may begin.

12. When 1 minute has passed, call time. Ask the partner 2s (those who were speaking):
- How did you feel, and why?

Make sure you hear from many people. Ask the following question if it isn't answered in the participants' responses:
- How many of you were able to tell your story well?

Most people will respond that they could not tell their story well because they felt like no one was listening to them. Say:
- We help people be good storytellers and communicators by listening to what they have to say with more than our ears.

TryThis

Ask a volunteer to sit in your chair and talk about something—anything. Direct the participants to communicate through their body language that the person in the chair is the most interesting person they have ever listened to. Watch what the participants do with their bodies, and encourage them to change their postures, facial gestures, and eye contact until you think that they have really communicated interest. Then ask, "What did you need to do to show you were really listening?"

Next instruct the participants to show interest using just their eyes. Because you will see all their responses, you will need to tell the participants what the group is doing—winking, raising their eyebrows, making good eye contact, and so on.

Continue by asking everyone to show interest using the following body parts in turn: the mouth, the whole face, the hands, the shoulders, and the whole body.

An Overview of Attending Skills (10 minutes)

1. Pull up a chair at the front of the room, and ask the participants to gather nearby, facing you.

2. Ask the participants:
- What do you know now about using good attending skills?

Recruit a volunteer to record everyone's answers on newsprint. Ask the participants to be specific in answering the question. You are looking for answers such as maintaining good eye contact, smiling, nodding, and leaning in toward the speaker.

3. Distribute handout 25. Offer the following suggestions:
- Good listeners practice using good attending skills—eye contact, good facial gestures, and good body language. Good listeners recognize they play an important role in helping another person tell his or her story by being a good audience.
- Good listeners use small words and phrases—"Aha," "Wow," "Really," "Great"—(called minimal encouragers) to let the other person know they are listening.
- Good listeners know it takes energy and concentration to really listen well, and they make that sacrifice for others.

4. Ask the participants to go back to their partner from the previous activity. Give the following instructions for round 5:
- Partner 1, for this round you will be the speaker. Partner 2, you will be the listener.
- Partner 1, your job is to tell your partner about a great day in your life. It doesn't have to be the best day of your life, just a day you remember fondly.
- Partner 2, your job is to listen by using all the good attending skills you have just learned. Do your best to communicate nonverbally that you are really interested in the story the other person is telling.
- Are there any questions? [Address any questions.] You may begin.

5. After 1 minute has passed, call time. Ask the partner 1s (those who were speaking):
- How did you feel, and why?

Make sure you hear from many people. Ask the following question if it isn't answered in the participants' responses:
- How many of you were able to tell your story well?

Most people will respond that they could tell their story well because they felt like their partner was listening to them. Say:
- By giving people the attention they deserve, we give them an important gift. We give them the opportunity to share a part of themselves with us. That is a unique and special opportunity that we can give—and we can give it every time we listen to another person.

Attending Skills

Attending skills involve total presence. To tend to the person before you is to care enough to work at being as present as possible to her or him.

Posture

- Maintain a state of relaxed alertness.
- Incline your body toward the speaker—"sit on the edge of your seat."
- Face the speaker squarely—don't turn a cold shoulder.
- Keep your arms and legs uncrossed—keep your body open.
- Maintain an appropriate distance from the speaker—not too close or too far.

Body Movement

- Move your body in response to the speaker—by nodding your head, and so forth.
- Avoid making distracting motions or gestures.
- Do not respond to outside things that could distract you from the speaker.

Eye Contact

- Maintain fairly constant eye contact with the speaker.
- Allow your eyes to convey emotion to the speaker.

Facial Gestures

- Use your face to communicate with the speaker—offer smiles, quizzical looks, winks, and so on.
- Avoid "hard" or angry looks.

Environment

- Reduce environmental distractions to a minimum.

Overview

True listening requires being present to the speaker by seeking to fully understand what he or she is sharing. Learning to reflect content, feeling, and meaning will further equip the young people for servant leadership. This minisession gives the participants an opportunity to learn and practice reflective listening skills.

Outcomes

◆ The participants will learn how to become better listeners.
◆ The participants will practice reflective listening skills.

Core Session: Reflective Listening Skills (30 minutes)

Preparation

- Gather the following items:
  - ❏ blank paper, one sheet for every three or four participants
  - ❏ pens or pencils
  - ❏ resource 7, "The Art of Reflective Listening"
  - ❏ one copy of resource 8, "How Was Your Day?" cut apart as scored
  - ❏ copies of handout 26, "Reflecting Listening Skills," one for each participant
- Review resource 7 to prepare yourself to conduct this session.
- Ask the first six participants who arrive to take one of the roles listed on resource 8. Give each of them the role description cut from the resource, and invite them to practice saying, "How was your day?" with the tones or feelings suggested on their sheets of paper.

"How Was Your Day?" (10 minutes)

1. Introduce the session by saying:

- In this session we are going to focus on listening skills by learning how to reflect the content, feelings, and meanings of what others say.

2. Form small groups of three or four participants. Give a sheet of blank paper and a pen or a pencil to each small group.

3. Ask the six volunteers to come up one at a time, stand in front of everyone, and present the line, "How was your day?" following the instructions they were given (from resource 8). After each one says the line, direct the small groups to guess and then write down the underlying emotion.

4. When the six participants have finished, encourage the groups to share their guesses as to the underlying emotions. Ask the six volunteers to identify the emotions they were attempting to present.

Reflective Listening Skills (10 minutes)

1. Share the following comments with the participants:

- The same phrase, "How was your day?" was said by each volunteer, but each person's body language, posture, and tone indicated a different message and feeling.

2. Offer some clear examples of how the presentations indicated emotions (for example: "Sue's whole body leaned forward, her face looked angry, her tone was upsetting—this was clearly an angry way of asking, 'How was your day?' I do not think I would want to respond to her!") Then say:

- Researchers claim that communication is 55 percent body language, 38 percent tone, and 7 percent actual words (Mehrabian, "Communication Without Words").
- Think about how those aspects of communication were expressed when each line was presented.

3. Connect the examples with reflective listening skills by distributing handout 26 and reviewing it with the participants.

Practicing Reflective Listening (10 minutes)

1. Assign each small group one type of reflective listening from handout 26.

2. Tell two personal stories, illustrating two situations from the list that follows. Spend about 2 minutes on each story. After each story, invite each small group to respond using the reflective listening skill assigned to it. If a group struggles to use its skill correctly, invite the other groups to suggest an appropriate response.

- a difficult decision you made
- a really great friend or a favorite teacher
- why you enjoy working with youth
- the kindest thing anyone has ever done for you

3. Summarize the session by saying:

- Servant leaders spend a significant amount of time listening to others. For people to trust you and to follow your lead, they need to feel understood by you.
- It takes time to learn how to listen with our hearts, minds, and bodies. It takes skill to fully hear what another person is saying.
- Listening well is an important element of Christian leadership. We often want to speak and get our point across. Before we do, however, we must listen to others to ensure we understand what they are trying to tell us.

The Art of Reflective Listening

Although we spend much of our waking life interpreting the world around us, we can miss important pieces of information if we are not actively listening. Listening requires emptying ourselves of our preoccupations and of the need to be working on our response while the other is speaking. Listening includes interpreting, finding meaning in, and understanding the significance of what is being said.

As we actively listen, we must ensure that what we are interpreting is correct. The skills for accomplishing that are called *reflective listening* skills. When we listen reflectively, we act as a mirror to the one speaking. We respond to the speaker by *reflecting* what the person has said. Reflective listening has four levels: paraphrasing, reflecting feelings, reflecting meaning, and summary reflection. See handout 26, "Reflective Listening Skills," for an explanation of each.

Reflective listening is a way of checking in with the speaker to ensure that we have the correct meaning (including content, feeling, and significance of what is being said), as well as communicating to the speaker that we are truly listening.

Initially, practicing reflective listening skills may feel awkward and phony. With repetition, however, they will feel more genuine, and reflective listening will become a natural way of being present to others. During this session, explain that to the participants so that they are encouraged to continue practicing reflective listening skills beyond the session and will not get discouraged by the initial difficulty of integrating the skills into everyday conversation.

Here are three resources that address positive communication skills, including reflective listening:

- Bolton, Robert. *People Skills: How to Assert Yourself, Listen to Others, and Resolve Conflicts.* New York: Touchstone Books, 1979.
- Covey, Sean. *The Seven Habits of Highly Effective Teens.* New York: Simon and Schuster, 1998.
- Covey, Stephen R. *The Seven Habits of Highly Effective People.* New York: Simon and Schuster, 1990.

By definition, leadership is not an isolated process. Leadership automatically includes others. Christian leadership adds the element of service to the call of leadership. Christian leaders must develop the art of listening so that they can be deeply present to the ones they serve and the ones with whom they serve. Few things build trust as well as the satisfaction of being understood. Good reflective skills help young people develop the ability to seek first to understand and be present to those around them.

"How Was Your Day?"

1. When the leader invites you to the front, say the line, "How was your day?" in a happy way. Use your tone, emotions, and body to express that.

2. When the leader invites you to the front, say the line, "How was your day?" in an angry way. Use your tone, emotions, and body to express that.

3. When the leader invites you to the front, say the line, "How was your day?" in a disappointed way. Use your tone, emotions, and body to express that.

4. When the leader invites you to the front, say the line, "How was your day?" in a sarcastic way. Use your tone, emotions, and body to express that.

5. When the leader invites you to the front, say the line, "How was your day?" in a tired way. Use your tone, emotions, and body to express that.

6. When the leader invites you to the front, say the line, "How was your day?" in a frightened way. Use your tone, emotions, and body to express that.

Reflective Listening Skills

Reflective listening skills provide a mirror to the person speaking. The idea is to reflect what the person is saying. Reflective listening includes four levels:

- **Paraphrasing** is a short response that affirms the content of what the speaker was saying. Paraphrasing says the same thing the speaker is saying, using the listener's words. It ensures that the listener is hearing the message correctly.

- **Reflecting feelings** is a response that focuses not just on content but also on underlying feelings. The listener concentrates on the body language, tone, and feeling words used by the speaker. Statements that reflect feelings can begin with "You feel sad because . . ."

- **Reflecting meaning** is a response that suggests a possible meaning being conveyed. The listener expresses it as an invitation for clarification. Using this response is a way for listeners to make sure that they are correct in their assumption about underlying feelings and tone. Statements that reflect meaning can begin with "It sounds like you are . . ."

- **Summary reflection** is a response whereby the listener summarizes what she or he has heard the speaker say—not the listener's opinion on the issue. Summary reflection is used to let the speaker know that she or he is understood. Summary reflections may begin with "What I have heard you saying is . . ."

Group
Decision-Making Skills

17

Overview

Decision making is part of leadership and part of planning. This session helps young leaders understand how to use different decision-making methods when leading groups in planning.

Outcomes

◆ The participants will be introduced to different styles of decision making.
◆ The participants will learn a process for group decision making.

Core Session:
Decision-Making Skills (45 minutes)

Preparation

- Gather the following items:
  - ❑ copies of handout 27, "Winter Ball Parenting," one for each participant
  - ❑ pens or pencils
  - ❑ newsprint and markers
  - ❑ copies of handout 28, "Styles of Decision Making," one for each participant
  - ❑ copies of handout 29, "A Decision-Making Process," one for each participant

Winter Ball Parenting (35 minutes)

1. Welcome the participants, and introduce the topic by saying:

- As leaders, you are called on to make decisions. Sometimes leaders are asked to make decisions for their groups. Sometimes leaders make a decision in consultation with their groups. Sometimes they lead their groups in making a decision together. Learning more about decision making can help you in all those situations.

2. Distribute handout 27, and pens or pencils. Give the following instructions:

- Imagine that all the parents of the students at your high school have agreed to follow the same parenting style for their children attending the winter ball. This dance is open to all high school–aged youth and is held between Christmas and New Year. The parents have decided that all the young people who go to the dance will be given the same rules, curfews, and information.
- Now imagine that you are allowed to choose the style of parenting.
- Remember, all the parents will have to follow this style—regardless of the specific situation or circumstances of each young person.
- The style you choose will be used by everyone—including teenagers who are trustworthy and those who look for ways to get around rules. The rules will be the same for teenagers who have been dating for a long time and for those on their first date.

- On the handout you will find five strategies for how parents could handle their children who are attending the ball.
- Read all the strategies. Then rank them by putting the letter of your first choice on the line above the 1, the letter of your second choice on the line above the 2, and so on, all the way to 5 for the style that you believe is the least appropriate.

  Give the participants a few minutes to make their decisions.

3. Tell the participants that this part of the activity introduces *voting* as a style of decision making. Say:

- Raise your hand if strategy A was your number 1 selection.

  Write the number of participants who chose A on newsprint. Do the same for B, C, D, and E. Determine which two choices received the most votes.

4. Announce the two strategies that received the most votes, and tell the participants they now must vote for one of those two. Call out the letter of one of those strategies, and ask the participants to raise their hands to vote for that strategy. Record on newsprint the number of participants who choose that strategy. Repeat the voting for the other strategy. Announce the winner.

5. In the large group, discuss the following questions:

- How comfortable are you with having all the parents use this style of parenting?
- Do you think it is the best choice? Why or why not?
- What are the advantages of voting? [Some possible answers are that everyone gets to participate, it does not take long, and it seems fair.]
- What are the disadvantages of voting? [Some possible answers are that the majority may not like the final decision, there is no room for discussion, and people may not support the decision.]

6. Make the following points about voting as a decision-making style:

- We are used to voting in this country, but it is not always the best style of decision making. As we have seen in presidential elections, sometimes the vote is so close that almost half the people involved feel that they lost when the final decision is announced.
- Voting does work well when a very large group of people want or need to be involved in making a decision, and the decision does not demand that everyone support it.
- Voting can be used as a part of decision making—to narrow down choices before talking about the best decision.

7. Tell the participants that this part of the activity introduces *consulting* as a decision-making style. Then select the oldest youth participant to help you. Explain that for the purposes of this part of the activity, the person you chose is the authority. Ask the recruit to come forward with his or her handout. Explain the activity this way:

- I have selected [name of recruit] to be the authority. [Name of recruit] has lived longer than the rest of you and is therefore more knowledgeable about parenting styles, having been parented the longest.

Ask the authority what he or she recorded for a ranking. Write the ranking on a sheet of newsprint for all to see (for example, "D, A, C, B, E"). Then say:

- Sometimes authorities are asked to make decisions all by themselves, but often they consult others.
- When consulting, both parties—the authority and those consulted— should be open to change.

8. Invite the participants to give the authority some of their insights about the different parenting styles. Ask the participants to be specific about why they made the choices they did. After each person speaks, make sure the authority has an opportunity to ask a question or to provide additional insight into what they were thinking. You might begin the consultation by asking the participants:

- If you had a different first choice than the authority, can you explain why you thought it was the best parenting style for the winter ball?

Give the group about 3 minutes for this consultation process, and make sure that you hear from a variety of people.

9. Offer everyone (the authority and the rest of the participants) an opportunity to reconsider their ranking as a result of the consultation. Give them a minute or two to make any changes they want to make; point out that they do not have to make changes. When everyone is done, ask the authority to give his or her new ranking. If it differs from the authority's first ranking, print it on the newsprint.

10. Make the following points about consulting as a decision-making style:

- Often authorities get to make decisions. Who are some authorities in your lives? [Some possible answers are parents, teachers, principals, pastors, and coaches.]
- What is the difference between an authority and an expert? [Answers should include the following points: An authority is in a position of power, but is not necessarily an expert. An expert has some specific skill or knowledge. Some authorities are also experts, but not every authority is an expert.]

- When is it good to allow authorities to make decisions? [Some possible answers are when time is short, when the authorities are also experts, and when the whole group cannot be gathered to make the decision.]
- When is it not good to have authorities make decisions? [Some possible answers are when the group could make a better decision together and when everyone has to support the decision.]
- [If the top choice selected by the authority is different from the one selected by voting, ask:] How comfortable are you with having all the parents use this style of parenting?

11. Introduce *consensus* as a style of decision making by saying the following things:

- A third style of decision making is called consensus. It involves the whole group working together to make a decision. It is similar to consultation, except that no one person is responsible for making the final decision. Everyone in the group must make the decision together, by sharing ideas and opinions.
- Consensus is effective only if everyone is willing to work together and is open to the thoughts and ideas of others. Consensus is effective when people believe that the best decision will be made from the wisdom of the whole group.

12. Distribute handout 28. Run through the rules, benefits, and drawbacks of consensus. Make the following points:

- Consensus takes more time than the other decision-making styles, but it often produces the best result.
- True consensus means everyone fully supports a decision. There is also limited consensus, which means everyone is able to live with a decision. In a limited consensus, the group members agree that a decision is the best they will be able to come up with and that they are willing to support it.
- Use consensus when a decision is worth the time and energy, and it is really important that everyone have ownership of the decision.

A Decision-Making Process (10 minutes)

1. Distribute handout 29. Then say:

- There is a process for gathering information, selecting options, and making a decision.

2. Talk through the group decision-making process on the handout, using this example:

1. *Identify the decision to be made.* Your parish wishes to participate in a weeklong summer mission experience that costs $350 for each person

who attends. The parish would like to send six young people and two adults for the week.

2. *Determine the available options.* Brainstorming produces four funding options for those who will participate in the experience:

- ask for donations as a group
- raise the money themselves through donations and through family or personal funds
- conduct a big fund-raiser
- ask the parish to pay

3. *Choose the three most workable options.* The participants choose these three:

- ask for donations as a group
- raise the money themselves
- conduct a big fund-raiser

4. *Discuss the advantages of each option.*

- Asking for donations lets lots of people be involved in supporting the youth and could be accomplished without a lot of time and energy.
- Raising the money themselves would emphasize the importance of working for and toward a goal and the necessity for self-sufficency.
- Conducting a big fund-raiser could be a good community builder, and could give donors something for their money.

Discuss the disadvantages of each option.

- Asking for donations does not encourage a sense of independence or self-sufficiency.
- Raising the money themselves does not allow for the community to be involved or supportive of the young people's efforts
- Fund-raising might interfere with other parish efforts and could take a lot of work.

5. *Decide which decision to implement.* The participants choose to ask for donations.

6. *Evaluate the decision.* After the experience, the participants discuss these questions:

- Did the donation campaign involve the rest of the parish?
- Did it take a lot of time?
- Did it raise the money needed?

3. (If you will do the practice round from the session extension, move to that activity now and then return to this step.) Summarize the decision-making process by saying:

- It is important to know a process for making good decisions. When we pay attention to the steps we have covered here, we can make better decisions.

- We might find that we use many different styles of decision making within this process. We might vote to narrow down the list of possible solutions, we might try to reach consensus on the final decision, or we might consult an authority about the situation and possible options.
- This process obviously works for group decisions, but it is also good for personal decisions. Consider using it when making important decisions like what college to go to, what type of summer job to pursue, and where to go on a family vacation.

Session Extension

Practicing the Decision-Making Process (20 minutes)

Lead this activity after you have completed step 2 of the preceding activity, "A Decision-Making Process."

1. Form small groups of four to six participants. Give the following instructions:
- You have been asked to organize a fun night for the sixth-grade students in the parish.
- The pastor has given you two criteria: first, the event cannot cost anything, and second, it must be held in the parish hall.
- Your job is to use the decision-making process to create a plan for the fun night. Follow the process on the handout, using the style or styles of decision making (voting, consulting, or consensus) that work best for your group. You can jot notes for each step of the process on the handout as you go.
- You will have 15 minutes to make your decision.

2. If time allows, invite each small group to present its program idea. This will take an additional 10 minutes.

3. Use the closing comments from step 3 of the preceding activity, "A Decision-Making Process."

Winter Ball Parenting

Read all the strategies described on this handout. Then rank them by putting the letter of your first choice on the line above the **1** below, the letter of your second choice on the line above the **2**, and so on, all the way to **5** for the style that you believe is the least appropriate.

_____   _____   _____   _____   _____
1   **2**   **3**   **4**   **5**

Strategy A

The parents should not give their children curfews, or chaperone the ball and the after-ball activities; they also should not ask too many questions before or after the event. Students who get in trouble that night should figure out how to get themselves out of trouble.

Strategy B

The parents can talk to their children before the ball about concerns they have regarding behavior, but they should not provide a curfew. The students will have to tell their parents what their after-ball plans are and when they will be returning home. The parents should be called if there is trouble; the parents will respond, but there will be no consequences for the students.

Strategy C

Because the ball will end at midnight, the curfew for the students will be 2 a.m. The parents will provide rides to and from the ball and any after-ball activities. Any after-ball activity must be chaperoned by at least two parents. Any child who breaks one of these rules will be grounded for three weeks.

Strategy D

The parents can be involved in the preparations for and discussions about the ball, but they should not try to have input into their children's decisions. The parents can chaperone the ball and the after-ball activities, but only to share in the pleasure of the event. Unless someone is going to get killed or is going to hurt someone else, the parents should stay out of the way. The curfew for everyone will be 3 a.m., and the students are free to call their parents to renegotiate the curfew if they are going to be late.

Strategy E

The parents should talk with their children about how they expect them to behave. The curfew will be 2 a.m. The parents are welcome to drive or chaperone their children. After-ball events must be cleared with the parents. The parents should be called in the event of trouble. They will respond, and there will be consequences for the students. The parents are free to punish their children if they believe that is necessary.

Styles of Decision Making

Voting

How It Works
- For a simple majority, the choice with the most votes wins.
- For a true majority, the winning choice must receive at least 50 percent of the votes plus one.

Advantages
- Voting is fast, is easy, requires no discussion, and works well with large numbers of people.

Disadvantages
- Group members may feel like winners or losers, and those who lost may not support the decision.

When It Should Be Used
- Voting should be used when time is short, when the decision does not require that everyone be happy with it, when the group is very large and discussion is impractical, and when it is necessary to narrow down choices before discussing options.

Consulting

How It Works
- For decision by authority, one person makes the choice for the group.
- For decision by authority with consultation, one person makes the choice after giving members of the group an opportunity to provide input.

Advantages
- Decision by authority is fast, is easy, and does not require discussion.
- Decision by authority with consultation allows input from group members and allows them to feel listened to, and gives the authority additional information to consider.

Disadvantages

- The group may not feel ownership for the decision and may not use their energies to act on it. They can resent the power of the authority.
- In decisions by authority with consultation, if the authority makes a different decision than that supported by the input of the group members, bad feelings and resentment can occur. Feelings of ownership among members is not guaranteed.

When It Should Be Used

- Consulting should be used when the authority has some expertise and information not shared by the members, for routine matters and decisions that will not need a strong ownership of group members, and when there is little time or opportunity to talk with group members.

Consensus

How It Works

- For consensus, everyone expresses their ideas and opinions; no one judges or asserts power over the group. People deal with the facts and information necessary to make a good decision, and stay away from opinions and personality conflicts. People do not give up their ideas to avoid conflict. In fact, they understand that conflict is inevitable and helpful for finding out new information and ideas. The group continues working until each member can support or at least live with the decision.
- For true consensus, everyone fully supports the idea.
- For limited consensus, everyone can live with the idea.

Advantages

- Consensus produces a decision that everyone is happy with and is usually very creative, results in a decision that group members are highly committed to, uses the resources of the whole group, and results in no losers.

Disadvantages

- A lot of time and energy is required, and the group members must be committed to reaching consensus or a false consensus can occur (in a false consensus, people pretend to agree with the decision but are not committed to it). The group members must have good listening and negotiating skills to reach a successful consensus.

When It Should Be Used

- Consensus should be used when the decision is worth the time and the energy, and ownership for the idea by everyone is important.

A Decision-Making Process

Leaders are responsible for decisions that require great thought and effort. Having a game plan for tackling those decisions is important because they affect the people with whom we interact. By developing and using good decision-making skills, we avoid unnecessary conflict. Decision making is the process of naming issues, identifying options, choosing solutions, and implementing decisions within the framework of our vision, values, and priorities.

1. **Identify the decision to be made.**
   Describe the situation clearly so that you can recognize what the real issue is:

2. **Determine the available options.**
   It is good to brainstorm several solutions without rejecting any. This is the opportunity for creative ideas to surface. Briefly name the options:

3. **Choose the three most workable options from the list you have brainstormed.**
   Option 1:

   Option 2:

   Option 3:

4. Discuss the advantages and disadvantages of each option.

Through this discussion, a picture of *why* one option might be more suitable than another will emerge. Respect each person's opinion during this step. Encourage participants to name their tangible and moral- or value-driven concerns.

	Advantages	**Disadvantages**
Option 1:		
Option 2:		
Option 3:		

5. Decide which decision to implement.

When you have explored your options and looked at the advantages and the disadvantages of each one, some things should start to fall into place. It is time to make a decision:

6. Evaluate the decision.

Set aside time for a future follow-up discussion to evaluate progress. This is important because learning and growth often happen in hindsight or while "working out the bugs." Look to make sure that the idea chosen yields the advantages you were hoping for.

Effective Meeting Skills

Overview

Anyone who has spent a lot of time at meetings knows that an effectively conducted meeting can make all the difference in how much is accomplished, in how well the attendees work together, and in how the attendees feel about their work. This session introduces the participants to some of the roles and structures that make a meeting run well.

Outcomes

◆ The participants will be introduced to roles and structures that make meetings effective.

◆ The participants will use skills and information to plan an effective meeting.

Core Session:
Effective Meeting Skills (35 minutes)

Preparation

- Gather the following items:
  - ❑ newsprint and markers
  - ❑ copies of handout 30, "How to Plan a Meeting," one for each participant
  - ❑ copies of handout 31, "A Sample Form for Taking Minutes," one for each participant
  - ❑ copies of handout 32, "A Checklist for Effective Meetings," one for each participant

Meeting Chaos (10 minutes)

1. Begin by welcoming the participants. Introduce the topic by saying:

- Meetings are a necessary part of life. People gather at meetings to make decisions, assign tasks, talk through ideas, plan for the future, and do many other things that cannot happen when people are not together.
- All of us have probably been to meetings that have been great and also to meetings that have left us feeling frustrated.
- Today we will take time to learn more about what makes a meeting effective.
- It is easier to make meetings good when we are in charge of them, but we can suggest changes to meetings when others are leading them.

2. Ask the participants the following questions and record their answers on newsprint in two columns, one headed "Bad" and the other "Good." If you have a good story to share about a bad meeting you have attended, you could tell it to help get the group thinking. Make sure you do not name specific people or groups.

- Think about the worst meeting you ever attended. What are some things that happened that you did not like? [List those in the "Bad" column.]
- Now think about the very best meeting you ever attended. What are some elements that made that meeting effective and a good experience? [List those in the "Good" column.]

3. Summarize the feedback from the participants and then offer these comments:

- The meeting facilitator has the responsibility to avoid the things listed in the "Bad" column and to do the "Good" things so that those attending can have a positive experience.
- The meeting facilitator can do some specific things to conduct a well-run meeting. Those skills can be used in youth ministry, school organizations, or any setting where planning meetings take place.

Meeting Skills (25 minutes)

1. Form seven small groups. Give each participant a copy of handout 30, and assign each group one of the meeting elements listed on the handout. (If there are fewer than fourteen participants, form as many groups of three or four as possible, and ask some groups to work on more than one element.) Also give copies of handout 31 to the members of the "Role Assignments" group, who should distribute handout 31 to all participants during their presentation.

2. Give the following instructions:

- Your group has been assigned one component to consider when planning an effective meeting. Your job, as a group, is to review the information provided, and then choose a way to present that information to the rest of the participants. You can be as creative as you like, but you must do an accurate job of presenting the core content that you have been assigned.
- The group that has been given the "Role Assignments" element should incorporate the information from handout 31 into its presentation.
- You are free to put the information about your assigned element in your own words.
- You have only 7 minutes to read your information and prepare your presentation.

As the groups are working, move among them to answer questions.

3. Beginning with the first meeting element on handout 30, invite each small group to make its presentation.

4. When all the groups have presented, summarize their work and add anything they have missed. Include the following thoughts:

- If a meeting planner is attentive to each of these elements, the meeting will be more effective.
- Good meetings are possible when there is a skilled facilitator and skilled meeting participants. [If you have already taught the group-facilitation skills in chapter 11, "Leading Group Discussions," refer to those skills.]

5. Distribute handout 32. Highlight the things on the checklist that your particular group struggles with the most. Be sure to emphasize things that speak to the leaders of the meetings and the participants. For instance, if you have trouble with lots of people talking at once at meetings, stress the point "Everyone has an opportunity to present their viewpoints." If meetings run long, highlight "The meeting has a scheduled ending time that is honored." Then ask:

• What will we need to do differently (as members and leaders) to run more effective meetings? [List the responses on newsprint.]

Note: If this session is being done with people who regularly meet together, make sure they are specific in naming changes for their meetings.

6. Conclude with these comments:

• Together we can help one another lead more effective meetings. Use what you have learned in this session when you are leading or participating in a meeting at the parish, in the school, or in the community.

• [If the participants will be meeting with you as a group for planning purposes:] I will remind you of this information in the future if our youth ministry meetings get off track or if you do not use the skills we have covered.

How to Plan a Meeting

Consider the following elements when planning a meeting.

Purpose

Name the three most important things you hope to accomplish. The purpose for a meeting might include these points:
- planning or assigning tasks
- connecting or building community
- completing a specific task
- learning or training
- socializing
- faith sharing, prayer, or reflection

Timing

When determining how long the meeting should last, consider these questions:
- Can we realistically cover the agenda?
- Will the group have enough energy for the agenda?
- When will the meeting start?
- When will it end?
- What is the best time to meet, as determined by these concerns:
  - availability
  - energy
  - impact on other activities

Participants

Consider whether you have invited the following people:

- those who have the authority to decide issues
- those whose commitment is needed
- those who need to know

With meetings focused on long-term planning, event planning, and the completion of specific tasks, strive for the minimum number of people because smaller numbers hold interest and increase participation.

Agenda

An agenda serves as a road map to keep discussions focused and work moving ahead. *Before the meeting,* decide what needs to be included (focus on your main objectives, the purpose that you have identified for the meeting). Consider the following questions:

- What has to be accomplished? (tasks)

- What is important about the relationships of the members? (maintenance of relationships)

- What items need to be considered for these areas:
  - ❑ discussion
  - ❑ reports
  - ❑ decisions
  - ❑ recommendations

- What prayers, new business, introductions, and other elements are needed?

After you have created a written agenda, complete these tasks:
- Distribute the agenda before the meeting so that the participants will know what to expect.
- Review and adapt the agenda at the beginning of the meeting as needed.
- Review the agenda at the end of the meeting, highlighting items that were not covered and tabling them until the next meeting.

Physical Arrangements

Consider the following questions:
- What facilities and equipment does the meeting need?

- How should the meeting room be arranged?
  - Can everyone see one another?

  - Are tables needed for written work?

  - Is the room large enough or small enough to comfortably hold those in attendance?

Role Assignments

Every meeting should include three roles:
- The **facilitator** leads the meeting, guides the conversations, and keeps the group on task. One or more people can play this role during a meeting.
- The **recorder** documents the discussions and the decisions made by the group. After the meeting the recorder provides a written report of the meeting to all those who participated, keeping a copy for reference at future meetings. The recorder should not be the same person as the facilitator.

- The **timekeeper** ensures that the meeting starts and ends on time. The timekeeper also makes sure that the group does not spend too much time on any one agenda item. Sometimes the facilitator plays this role during a meeting.

In addition, consider these roles:

- setup and cleanup
- hospitality
- prayer leader
- presenter

Follow-up Methods

Meetings often lead to additional tasks being assigned for completion in the coming weeks or months. At the end of the meeting, it is important to know the following:

- what tasks have been assigned to whom
- the deadlines for completion of those tasks
- who is accountable to whom

Also be sure to give a summary of the meeting, including these elements:

- Describe the mutual understanding of decisions made, tasks assigned, and work completed.
- Identify items that need follow-up, and who will do the work.
- Identify any next steps and possible agenda items for the future.

You might also want to check in on these concerns:

- How are people feeling?
- Do people need anything (such as information, help, or supplies) to move forward?

(The material on this handout is adapted from *Effective Meeting Skills—A Practical Guide for More Productive Meetings,* by Marion E. Haynes [Menlo Park, CA: Crisp Publications, 1988], pages 26–27. Copyright © 1988 by Crisp Publications. Permission applied for.)

A Sample Form for Taking Minutes

Meeting dates: _____

People in attendance: _____

_____

_____

Meeting started at: (List the exact time the meeting started.) _____

Meeting ended at: (List the exact time the meeting ended.) _____

Agenda items: (For each agenda item, record the following information: what was discussed, any additional information that was needed, and decisions that were made. Indicate who will do what and when. You do not need to indicate in detail everything that is said, but you do need to give the major points that were discussed, for the benefit of those not present as well as for the group's memory.)

Agenda item 1: _____

_____

_____

Agenda item 2: _____

_____

_____

Agenda item 3: _____

_____

_____

Agenda item 4: _____

_____

_____

Decisions made:

	What is the decision?	Who is responsible for acting on it?	What is the deadline for its completion?
1			
2			
3			
4			
5			
6			

Future steps: (List any items that did not get covered on the agenda, any next steps that should be taken, and suggestions for future meetings.)

_____

_____

_____

_____

_____

Next meeting: (List when, where, and who.) _____

_____

_____

A Checklist for Effective Meetings

Review this checklist to ensure that you have thought through all the necessary elements of the meeting.

- ☐ The facilitator prepares an agenda before the meeting.
- ☐ The participants have an opportunity to contribute to the agenda.
- ☐ The facilitator provides notice of the meeting start time, end time, and location, and gives a copy of the agenda to each participant.
- ☐ Meeting facilities are confirmed and are comfortable and adequate for the number of participants.
- ☐ Beverages and food are available when appropriate. Water is always available.
- ☐ The meeting begins on time.
- ☐ The meeting has a scheduled ending time that is honored.
- ☐ The facilitator or timekeeper monitors time throughout the meeting.
- ☐ Everyone has an opportunity to present their viewpoints.
- ☐ No one dominates the discussion.
- ☐ Everyone has a voice in decisions made at the meeting.
- ☐ The meeting ends with a summary of accomplishments.
- ☐ The group defines and delegates follow-up tasks, and sets dates for completion.
- ☐ The recorder ensures that each participant receives minutes of the meeting.
- ☐ The facilitator stays in touch with the participants, following up on actions agreed upon during the meeting.
- ☐ The decision-making process used is appropriate for the purpose and the size of the group.

(The material on this handout is adapted from *Effective Meeting Skills—A Practical Guide for More Productive Meetings,* by Marion E. Haynes [Menlo Park, CA: Crisp Publications, 1988], page 3. Copyright © 1988 by Crisp Publications. Permission applied for.)

19 Giving a Witness Talk

AT A GLANCE

Study It

Core Session:
Giving a Witness Talk
(40 minutes)

- ◆ Scripture Reflections
  (15 minutes)
- ◆ What Makes a Good
  Witness Talk?
  (10 minutes)
- ◆ How to Develop and
  Give a Witness Talk
  (15 minutes)

Overview

Witness talks can be used any time or place where sharing a faith journey could be a valuable experience. Adults, young adults, or young people can give witness talks. This session helps those who are giving a witness talk to prepare, and offers suggestions about what to include, as well as helpful hints for making the talk meaningful.

Outcomes

- ◆ The participants will learn how to prepare for and give a good witness talk.
- ◆ The participants will reflect on the importance of sharing their faith journey.

Core Session:
Giving a Witness Talk (40 minutes)

Preparation

- Gather the following items:
  - ❏ three sheets of blank paper
  - ❏ pens or pencils
  - ❏ *Catholic Youth Bible*s or other Bibles, one for every four participants
  - ❏ newsprint and markers
  - ❏ one copy of resource 9, "Scripture Reflections," cut apart as scored
  - ❏ copies of handout 33, "Developing and Giving Your Witness Talk," one for each participant

Scripture Reflections (15 minutes)

1. Begin with the following comments:

- We have gathered to discuss the steps involved in preparing a witness talk. The sharing of faith stories has a long history in our Church, and has played a meaningful role in the faith development of youth and adults throughout the centuries. The Bible, in part, is a witness story, and God continues to reveal himself to us within our own lives.

- We are going to start by looking at a few stories from the Bible to learn how to give witness, and why it is important.

2. Form three small groups. Give each group one of the Scripture passages and its reflection questions, from resource 9, and a Bible for every four participants. (If the number of people in this session is small, all the participants can work on the Scripture passages together—which will take longer—or you can choose one or two passages for the whole group to work on together.)

Ask each group to select a recorder, and provide each recorder with a sheet of blank paper and a pen or pencil. Direct each small group to read its assigned Scripture passage and to discuss the two questions that accompany it. Instruct the recorder in each small group to take notes. Give the groups about 7 minutes to read and discuss.

3. Ask the recorder from each group to report what was learned about witness talks from the Scripture passages. Add the following points and connect them with the participants' comments:

- *Acts 26:1–23.* The three movements in Paul's witness parallel current witness talks. Witness talks usually include sharing about the time before faith played a meaningful role in a person's life, then how faith came to be important in a new way, and finally how life is different because of faith.
- *John 4:4–42.* People giving witness talks make themselves familiar to those listening, are willing to listen to others' stories, share the Good News, and offer hope for the future (regardless of someone's past).
- *2 Cor. 4:5–10.* Sharing faith can be risky; however, Paul tells us it is not our own power that will make us good at sharing faith, but God's.

4. Offer the following comments:
- All witness talks should tell a story about God.
- Credible witnesses attempt to invite listeners to enter into their lives and welcome listeners to share their own stories of faith.
- If we trust, God will allow our words and thoughts to be about the Good News.

What Makes a Good Witness Talk? (10 minutes)

1. (If the majority of the participants have not heard a witness talk, skip this step and begin with step 2.) Direct the participants to find a partner—someone who is not from the group they worked with in the preceding activity, "Scripture Reflections." Instruct the participants to do this:
- Share with your partner about a great witness talk you have heard. Explain what made it meaningful to you.

    Give the participants about 5 minutes to share.

2. Gather the participants back into a large group. Record the answers to the following question on newsprint:
- What is something specific that was shared during a witness talk that made it meaningful to you?

For groups who have not heard a witness talk, ask:
- What makes someone a good storyteller?
- When someone talks about faith or religion, what makes it meaningful to you?

3. Summarize the participants' comments and add or emphasize the following points:
- A witness talk touches different people differently. The goal is to do the best job of telling your story and trust that God will do the rest.
- We can learn from the good things others do, but we cannot borrow their lives and stories. God is working in each of us, so we should concentrate our efforts on communicating the story of God in our lives.

TryThis

Before conducting this activity, invite someone who has previously given a witness talk (perhaps on a past retreat or in a faith-sharing session) to offer that talk to the group you have gathered. After the talk, invite the participants to discuss their experience as listeners and what made the talk meaningful to them.

How to Develop and Give a Witness Talk (15 minutes)

1. Distribute handout 33. Review the handout with the participants, spending about 3 minutes on each section. If the participants have limited experience with witness talks, add stories or personal experiences, if possible, to animate the points. If the participants have had experience either giving or hearing witness talks, invite them to add their own stories and experiences.

2. Encourage the participants to ask questions and to share insights, fears, and comments.

Scripture Reflections

Read Acts of the Apostles 26:1–23.

1. What are the key elements of Paul's witness talk to King Agrippa? (Hint: There are three separate parts to this reading: Acts of the Apostles 26:1–11,12–18,19–23.)
2. How might you talk about your faith in a witness talk?

Read John 4:4–42.

1. What does Jesus say and do with the Samaritan woman that make his message meaningful to her?
2. How might you talk about your faith in a witness talk?

Read 2 Corinthians 4:5–10.

1. What is the risk of witnessing?
2. What must you remember when preparing a witness talk?

Developing and Giving Your Witness Talk

Preparing

A good witness talk requires preparation. People who look like they are talking without benefit of notes or preparation are usually the most prepared. Most often, people take weeks to prepare, giving themselves time to think, pray, write, practice, get feedback, rewrite, and practice again. The following ideas can help you before you ever start the process of writing:

- **Know your subject matter.** Whether or not you have been given an outline or reflection questions to help you prepare, be sure to find out the following information:
  - What is the main theme of the talk?
  - What are three specific secondary themes or focuses that need to be addressed?
  - Do you need to tie the talk to a specific focus of the event at which you will give it?
  - What will the participants be doing before and after the talk?
  - Do you need to tie the talk into those activities?
- **Know how long you have.** The best witness talk is fifteen to twenty minutes long. You will have to make some good choices about what you will say and what you will not say.
- **If necessary, do some research.** If you have been asked to talk about something that goes beyond your own experience, consult others, read books or articles, search the Internet, and so on. For instance, if you have been asked to talk about Jesus and your relationship with him, you might want to read one of the Gospels so that you are familiar with the historical Jesus when you are preparing.
- **Reflect on the main theme.** Ask and answer questions related to the theme that come to your mind. Write down ideas and questions. Talk with others about your ideas. Pray! Tell God what you are thinking about and spend some time in silence to allow God to communicate with you. Let your ideas, prayers, and thoughts germinate for a while before you begin to write.
- **Consider an analogy.** You might begin with something like, "My faith life has been like a caterpillar becoming a butterfly because . . ." If you use an analogy, make sure that it helps tell your story in a meaningful way and

Handout 33: Permission to reproduce for program use is granted. © 2004 by Saint Mary's Press.

does not distract you. For example, if you use the caterpillar analogy, talk about life as a caterpillar, when and why you went into a cocoon state, what happened in that state to make you different, and what life is like as a butterfly. If you cannot easily do that, the analogy does not work for you, so either find a new analogy or do not use one.

- **Consider a scene from a movie or the lyrics of a song.** You can use a clip from a movie or a recording of a song, as long as it communicates what you want to say as well as or better than you could yourself. Also consider making your point by just referencing a movie scene or speaking the lyrics of a song.

- **There is no need to shock people.** Although some people have a "hit-bottom" experience that brings them to God, most come to experience God in the little things of life and through everyday experiences. Give an honest talk about your own experience, whatever that may be.

Writing

Take the time to write out your talk. That will help you find the right stories, the right details, and the images to communicate what you want. By writing it out, you can practice aloud, time your talk, and share it with others for comments and feedback. In writing your talk, remember the following points:

- Focus on a few things. If you try to say everything, you often end up saying too much, and people get lost in your words.
- Personal witness is the flesh of your talk, but you also need a skeleton. Make sure you achieve a good balance between the ideas you want to communicate (the skeleton) and the stories that bring it to life (the flesh).
- Use specific examples from your own life. Use only the necessary details to convey your message and make your point. Do not lose the message in the unnecessary details of a story.
- Plan your witness so that it flows smoothly from one point to another in a logical order.
- You can use quotations, Scripture passages, songs, and other resources when speaking, but make sure the majority of the talk comes from you.
- Do your best to witness to your faith without being preachy or giving the impression that you have it all together.
- Write as though you are telling a story to a friend.

Practicing

Practice your talk, and allow others to give you feedback. A story that you think is clear might need more details to make sense to someone else. Feedback will help you give the best possible witness talk and will help ensure that you will be understood by others.

Whenever possible, the program team for the event at which you will be speaking should listen to your witness talk and provide feedback. You should then have the opportunity to make changes and receive additional feedback. By taking time to practice with the program team, you can ensure that you have something valuable to share, and the program team can be sure the talk matches the other program elements. If this type of support is not available from the program team, find someone you trust and ask that person to work with you in preparing and practicing your talk.

Getting Ready

The final step before giving your talk is to get yourself, your notes, and your other materials ready.

- **Pray often.** When you are practicing, when you are thinking about your talk, and in the moments before giving it, pray often. If possible, ask someone to pray with you before giving your talk.
- **Write down your key points.** Most witness talks are not read. When you have practiced your talk enough times for it to be very familiar, write the key points (in words or sentences) on index cards. Some people can just write reminders of the flow from one story or idea to the next; others need an outline to work from. Remember that you may be nervous, so write down enough to remind you of what you wanted to say next, in case you forget.
- **Prepare any outside resources you are using.** Mark the page in a book, cue a song or a movie, have visuals handy, and so on.

Talking

When giving your talk, keep these hints in mind:

- Talk to the group in a relaxed and informal way. Remember that your task is to talk to and with people, not at them.
- Look at everyone and try to talk to each individual.
- Be yourself—as relaxed and natural as you can be.
- Allow your personality to come through—use your favorite phrases, laugh at your own stories, let people see the real you.
- Have confidence in yourself and in the witness that you have to share with others.

20 Knowing Youth

Overview

This session helps adult communities prepare for the participation and inclusion of youth in their groups or committees. It can be used with adults when a young person has been selected, appointed, or invited to participate on pastoral councils, in liturgy committees, in service committees, in parish outreach activities, in prayer groups, and so forth, or when youth will be participating with adults in the parish choir, liturgical ministries, or parish social events. It is designed to be 40 minutes long, so it can be used as part of a longer meeting, if desired.

Outcomes

◆ The participants will become aware of the emotions young people might experience when joining a group of adults.
◆ The participants will consider the unique insights youth bring to a community.
◆ The participants will plan for the inclusion and involvement of youth.

Core Session: Knowing Youth (40 minutes)

Preparation

- Gather the following items:
  - ❑ newsprint and markers
  - ❑ copies of handout 34, "Youth and Liturgy," one for each participant
  - ❑ copies of handout 35, "Working Side by Side with Youth," one for each participant
- Ask a volunteer to pray the opening prayer in step 2 of the activity "Remembering When."

Remembering When (10 minutes)

1. Begin this session by saying:

- Thank you for your willingness to spend some time preparing for the involvement of youth within your group or community.
- Young people have a right to participate in the life of the parish community, and equally have a baptismal responsibility to use their gifts well. However, it is not always easy for young people to participate alongside adults.
- In the time we have together, the goal is to discuss and plan for the successful inclusion and involvement of youth within your group or community.

2. Invite the volunteer you have selected to come forward and offer the following prayer:

> Loving God, you created all of us and gave us all different gifts.
> You call us to join together to become a sign of your love for the
>   world.
> Help us to learn about your young people, to appreciate their gifts,
>   support them, and share your love with them,
>   so that we may serve you and come to know you better.
> We ask this through Christ, our Lord and savior. Amen.

3. Urge the participants to think back to a time when they felt like they didn't belong, whether in a professional setting, a volunteer capacity, or a social situation. Instruct the participants to share with a partner what the situation was, and how they felt. Give the pairs about 3 minutes to share.

4. Gather the participants in a large group to discuss their experiences. Divide a sheet of newsprint into two columns. In the first column, record what made the participants feel as though they did not belong. In the second column, list the emotions they experienced.

5. From the information shared, ask the participants to guess which emotions the young people might also experience. Encourage the participants to name why the young people might feel like they will not belong. End this activity by saying:

- Adults who work with youth must try to lessen a young person's feelings of not belonging in order to offer the best opportunity for the young person to participate fully.

The Unique Gifts of Youth (10 minutes)

1. Distribute handout 34. Introduce this activity by saying:

- In 2002 the Center for Ministry Development and Saint Mary's Press, in collaboration with the National Federation for Catholic Youth Ministry, conducted a qualitative research study on the effective practices of Catholic youth ministry. The study provides insight into the thoughts and experiences of youth and adults and into effective ways of ministering with young people. This handout contains information from that study.

2. Form small groups of three or four participants. Invite each group to review the handout and then discuss the following two questions:

- What are the commonalities in the responses from young people and adults?
- What is unique to each group (adults and youth)?

Allow about 5 minutes for small-group sharing.

3. Regather as a large group and ask for feedback on the two questions. Note or emphasize that the young people in the study were alone in speaking about the sensual nature of liturgy and the need for liturgy to involve their bodies, hands, ears, eyes, and voices.

4. Conclude this activity by saying:

- Young people have a different way of experiencing the world—both because of their age and because of generational differences. The insights the young people provided about the need for liturgy to engage their senses is key to making liturgy as meaningful as possible to children and youth, and adults as well.
- Adolescents may be a small part of the overall parish population, but they are in a unique position of being able to speak for themselves and perhaps also for those younger than themselves.

- Young people often ask difficult questions, have unique insights, and can produce creative solutions to problems. When they feel safe to contribute to the work of a group, they can provide new energy and wisdom to the conversation. If we don't find ways to encourage their participation, we will lose the opportunity to grow because of their contributions.

Planning for Participation (20 minutes)

1. Distribute handout 35. Review with the participants the "Keys to Success" and "What You Might Want to Know About Youth" sections. Ask for comments or suggestions.

2. Invite the large group to spend 5 minutes discussing the questions listed under "Planning for Success" on the handout. Instruct the group to assign people to the tasks identified in those questions.

3. Direct the group to look over the "Some Things to Think About" section of the handout, and discuss the questions if necessary.

4. Conclude the session by saying:
- Thank you for taking the time to prepare for youth involvement in your group or committee.
- I am hopeful that the work we have done here will lead you and the young people to a positive experience.
- If you find that you need additional help in welcoming, including, or working with young people, please contact me.
- Thank you for being open to the gifts of youth.

Youth and Liturgy

What Youth Say

Vibrant liturgy engages the whole mind, body, and heart and connects us more deeply with community and strengthens our faith.

From the Interviews

"David praises the Lord leaping and dancing." The reason I know that is because of an '80s movie, but I know that is in there [the Bible]. Mass is supposed to be a sensual experience, not sensual in any sense that you might be thinking, but as in the five senses. We should be praising God with our entire bodies. With our hands, we need to clap. We need to sing. Mass should be joyful.

Saint Teresa of Ávila said, "Lord save me from stone-faced saints." Saints are joyful people, and I think we need to be more like them. God is on the altar, and if God walked right into this room, I think all of us would be amazed, and we would want to worship him with all of our body, with all of our senses, our mind, our being. And that's what I think we're trying to get at during the teen Mass, but I think the adults want us to remember where we are.

What Adults Say

Youth who are involved in liturgical roles bring a powerful presence and energy to the community, and the community takes pride and joy in the youth.

From the Interviews

The young people decided to interpret the Passion in relation to what is going on around us. For me, personally, it was a very powerful medium to convey and reach out to people about what suffering with Jesus Christ meant. The kids wrote the play, and it was based on the stations of the cross. It was all contemporary vignettes. It was really powerful.

I am also impressed when it comes to liturgy on Sunday morning. This is one parish where we have a tremendous number of high school students involved with service, both girls and boys. The pride they take in that, the confidence with which they are focused, the friendliness that they bring to it, and the respect that they have commanded from [others]. The parish is really proud of them.

What Youth Say

Leadership in liturgical ministry helps us uncover our gifts and experience affirmation for them, connects us with the community, and gives us a deeper understanding of what's being celebrated. Music uniquely adds to our ability to participate and engage fully in the liturgy.

From the Interviews

The way I interact and I strengthen and I show my faith is I play music. At church I go up there and I play bongos. I play drums, and it's just, the vibes I get when I'm done from the people—I helped make these people get up and dance, and shout, and clap their hands. It's this crazy vibe I get when everybody just has big smiles on their faces at the end of the song. Everyone is enjoying Mass.

At this church now I also do lectoring. It's not really a youth lector. I don't think there are any other youth lectors. Being one of the only youth lectors, it feels important because you get to represent the youth and their speaking skills with adults that are there.

I am a very musical person, so I think that is why it's a touchstone for me. But if you draw people in that way and then you pray together, and it's like—it's such a unique experience.

Our voices had lifted them up because everybody in the choir was crying too because we felt that God was helping us sing his praises.

What Adults Say

Good liturgy is a priority, and it includes music that is contemporary, homilies that youth can relate to, and youth as liturgical ministers.

From the Interviews

Another thing that is not working is the homily, the boring homily. To me, I think it's an insult to the young people, if they (priests) cannot be inclusive enough on a subject to include the entire parish. It should include the youth and the adults as well. If you want them to be part of the Church, then you need to talk to them while they are there. I think that is a big problem.

He came to church by himself when his parents really weren't practicing faith. He became a lector. He would memorize the whole reading himself. He would proclaim it without looking down. Somehow by putting the time into reading, it really nurtured his relationship with Christ. It is also a tremendous value to the community to see a young persons proclaim so well.

(The extracts from interviews on this handout are quoted from "Effective Youth Ministry Practices in Catholic Parishes" a joint research project of the Center for Ministry Development and Saint Mary's Press, in collaboration with the National Federation for Catholic Youth Ministry. The 2002 study is being published in *Effective Practices for Dynamic Youth Ministry* (Winona, MN: Saint Mary's Press, forthcoming).

Working Side by Side with Youth

Keys to Success

- Welcome the young people to the group or committee. Introduce the members to one another.
- Affirm the young people for their participation.
- Provide positive, honest feedback on ideas and insights. Not every idea a young person (or adult) contributes will be great or on target.
- Give the youth responsibility early and expect achievement. Let the youth learn from their mistakes, too.
- Recognize the gaps between the information, knowledge, and life experiences of youth and adults. Young people (and adults) need help, at times, filling those gaps.
- Invite the active participation of the young people by creating space and time for them to share their ideas.
- Share information about the way the group or committee operates. The young people will likely be nervous about participating if they perceive there are unwritten rules that need to be followed.
- Whenever possible, invite two or more young people to participate on an adult committee. One young person alone can be lost or isolated.
- Get parental support for youth involvement. Share with the parents information about the young people's role, the group, and the time commitment. Address any concerns the parents have. For instance, if schoolwork is suffering from overinvolvement, provide a break from participation in your group.
- Address issues related to age differences. For example: Will you all go by first names? Will the adults refrain from drinking alcohol at a social event or smoking cigarettes when youth are present?
- Be careful of stereotyping youth by age, appearance or clothing style, gender, ethnicity, or economic class.

What You Might Want to Know About Youth

- Young people often have less patience for the way something has always been done. They are likely to ask questions about traditions and to be interested in trying new ideas.
- Most young people have shorter attention spans and are comfortable with multitasking and working at a fast pace.
- Young people have different learning styles, so you may need to augment written and verbal communication with visual aids, add more experiential meeting elements, and break into small groups for discussions.
- Not all youth carry calendars with them. They may need a reminder phone call or e-mail a day or two before each meeting.
- Young people might have less formal knowledge but be more able than adults to name their lived experiences.
- Young people recognize when they are being patronized, and they resent being looked down upon. However, they appreciate efforts that help them share their experience or insight, as well as learn from other people's wisdom.
- Once they have formed relationships, young people have no problem participating fully. Previous generations were more conscious of the role of the elders than is this generation.
- Youth often come to evening meetings straight from after-school activities, sports practice, or work. Consider serving snacks at meetings to accommodate missed meals (and growing bodies).

Planning for Success

- How will you welcome the young people into your group? How will introductions be done?
- Is there background information the young people should have before the first gathering?
- Who will mentor the young people—provide knowledge, background information, and feedback and make reminder phone calls?
- What changes might you need to make to your meetings or gatherings to involve the young people more fully?

Some Things to Think About

- Are you willing to do things differently if the young people make suggestions that would invite change or if a modification would help a young person participate more fully?
- Are the meetings or gatherings life-giving for the adults who participate? If not, what should be changed before bringing in youth that would give everyone a better experience?

21

Knowing Adults

Overview

This session helps young people prepare for their participation in an adult community. It can be used when a young person has been selected, appointed, or invited to participate (on pastoral councils, in liturgy committees, in prayer groups, and so forth), or when young people will participate with adults in parish ministries or events (in choir, liturgical ministries, parish social events, and so forth).

Outcomes

◆ The participants will become aware of the emotions they might experience when joining a group of adults.

◆ The participants will consider the unique insights they can bring to a community and the importance of the gifts the adults bring to communal work as well.

◆ The participants will learn strategies to help them participate alongside adults.

Core Session:
Knowing Adults (40–70 minutes)

Preparation

- Gather the following items:
  - ❏ newsprint and markers
  - ❏ copies of handout 34, "Youth and Liturgy" (from chapter 20), one for each participant
  - ❏ a *Catholic Youth Bible* or other Bible, marked at 1 Cor. 12:12–21
  - ❏ copies of handout 2, "Parish Ministry Information Sheet" (from chapter 3), one for each parish ministry that the young people will be joining
  - ❏ copies of handout 3, "Leadership Tasks" (from chapter 3), one for each parish ministry that the young people will be joining
- Ask a volunteer to share the opening prayer in step 1 of the activity "Words of Wisdom."
- Before the session, contact the leaders of the parish committees, council, or groups that the young people will be joining. Ask them to complete and return to you handouts 2 and 3. Make copies of those completed handouts for distribution to the young people during the session, one copy for each participant who will be working with each group.

Words of Wisdom (10 minutes)

1. Begin by asking the volunteer to offer the following opening prayer:

Loving God, you created all of us and gave us all different gifts.
You call us to join together to become a sign of your love for the
    world.
Help us to learn about ourselves and our elders, to appreciate
    their gifts, support them, and share your love with them,
so that we may serve you and come to know you better.
We ask this through Christ, our lord and savior. Amen.

2. Ask the participants:

- How are you feeling about participating in a primarily adult group?

It will be best if you can name the specific groups they will be participating in. Listen for positive and negative emotions and for reasons behind those feelings.

3. Offer the following comments:

- I am excited that you will be involving yourself more fully with the adults of our parish. The adults you will be working with have much to share, and I am certain you will contribute great things to the group you will be working with.
- Today we are going to prepare you for participation with the adults of the community so that you will feel more comfortable participating fully within those groups and will be ready to contribute your gifts more fully to the parish community.

4. Ask the participants to think back to a time when they were starting something new (such as a school, a team, a peer group, or a youth ministry). Invite the participants to share with a partner what it was like to join the group, and what it was like to be part of the group after a while. Give the pairs about 3 minutes to share.

5. Divide a sheet of newsprint into two columns. Label one column "Then" and the other column "Now." Encourage the participants to name some things that happened, good or bad, when they were "the new kids." List their responses in the left column.

Ask:

- Did those experiences help you feel more comfortable or not?

Allow time for a few participants to respond. Then ask:

- What is it like for you now, or what was it like for you after you had been with the group for a while?
- What changed over time that made you feel more comfortable or less comfortable?

List their responses in the right column.

6. Ask the participants whether they can pick out any words of wisdom that they can share with one another as they enter into this new ministry in the parish. Some possible answers are "Change takes time," "Once you learn more about the group, you will feel more comfortable," "Try hard to fit in," and "Ask questions if you are unsure of something."

7. Conclude this activity by making the following comments:

- When starting something new, we can find it hard to know if we will fit in. You will probably feel awkward at first. You will want to remember your words of wisdom in the weeks ahead.
- [If you are preparing the adults for the participation of youth, perhaps through the use of chapter 20, "Knowing Youth," mention that here.]
- The next activity will help us recognize that both youth and adults have unique gifts to share with one another.

The Unique Gifts of Youth and Adults (15 minutes)

1. Distribute handout 34. Introduce this activity by saying:

• In 2002 the Center for Ministry Development and Saint Mary's Press, in collaboration with the National Federation for Catholic Youth Ministry, conducted a qualitative research study on the effective practices of Catholic youth ministry. The study provides insight into the thoughts and experiences of youth and adults and into effective ways of ministering with young people. This handout contains information from that study.

2. Form small groups of three or four participants. Invite the groups to review the handout and discuss the following questions:

• What excites you about what the youth said?

• What excites you about what the adults said?

Allow about 5 minutes for small-group conversation.

3. Ask for feedback on the two questions from the whole group. Continue by asking:

• Did you see anything different between what the youth said and what the adults said? If so, what? What was the same?

• Why is it important for your voice to be heard?

• Why is it important for adults to also have a voice?

• Which is more important—for your voice to be heard, or for adults to have a voice? [Hopefully, they will say both are important.]

4. Conclude the activity by offering the following comments:

• Each individual and every age-group makes important contributions in the life of our parish.

• You will be challenged at times to recognize the gifts or wisdom of others, and they may struggle to do the same for you, but that is what we are called to do as a Christian community.

• We are called to use our gifts, insights, and experiences to make things better. Listen to these words that Saint Paul wrote to the people of Corinth.

5. Read 1 Cor. 12:12–21. Then continue by saying:

• Because each of our gifts is important, we will take time to prepare for participation in adult communities.

Planning for Participation (10–40 minutes)

If you have enough time, complete both options 1 and 2. If you are short on time, complete only option 2.

Option 1: Skits (30 minutes)

1. Form small groups of four to six people. Give each group a sheet of newsprint and a marker. Ask each group to brainstorm a list of things about youth that might make adults hesitant about working with them. Allow about 5 minutes for the groups to complete their lists.

2. Invite each group to create and present a skit illustrating its "worst-case scenario" of young people. Give the participants just 2 minutes to come up with a skit in their small groups.

3. Allow each group to present its skit to the rest of the participants.

4. Ask each group to redo its skit by presenting a "best-case scenario" of young people. Give the groups 2 to 3 minutes to come up with their skits.

5. Allow each group to present its skit to the rest of the participants.

Option 2: Brainstorming (10 minutes)

1. Divide a sheet of newsprint into two columns. Label the first column "Don't" and the second column "Do." Invite the participants to think about what it means to participate with adults in a group or committee setting, and then brainstorm ideas for each column about what to do or not do when working with adults. Allow a few minutes for the participants to name the don'ts in the first column, and then the do's in the second column.

2. Conclude with these comments:
- It is not necessary for you become like the adults in order to fit in, nor should you expect them to become like you.
- Concentrate on the do's in this list and try to avoid the don'ts. As you get to know the other group members better, you will have more opportunities to reveal all that is unique about you. Remember, you want to make a good first impression!

Print Resources (5 minutes)

Give each participant a copy of every completed handout 2 and handout 3 that you have collected from the parish ministries. Instruct the young people to spend a minute or two reviewing the information. Address any questions. Conclude the session by saying:
- I am here to support your participation in our parish's life and ministry. Please let me know how things are going for you, and if there is any way I can help you.
- I am proud to have you represent the young people of our parish, and I trust that you will give this your best effort.

Acknowledgments

The scriptural quotations contained herein are from the New Revised Standard Version of the Bible, Catholic Edition (NRSV). Copyright © 1993 and 1989 by the Division of Christian Education of the National Council of the Churches of Christ in the United States of America. All rights reserved.

The material labeled *CFH* or *Catholic Faith Handbook* is from *The Catholic Faith Handbook for Youth,* by Brian Singer-Towns et al. (Winona, MN: Saint Mary's Press, 2004). Copyright © 2000 by Saint Mary's Press. All rights reserved.

The material labeled *CYB* or *Catholic Youth Bible* is from *The Catholic Youth Bible,* first edition (Winona, MN: Saint Mary's Press, 2004). Copyright © 2000 by Saint Mary's Press. All rights reserved.

The information about the goals and vision for ministry with adolescents on pages 9–10 is from, the words to ministry leaders and communities on page 20 are quoted from, and the statements in paragraphs 1–3 and 5–10 on handout 1 are from *Renewing the Vision: A Framework for Catholic Youth Ministry,* by the United States Conference of Catholic Bishops' (USCCB) Department of Education (Washington, DC: USCCB, 2002), pages 1–2, 42, 9, 11, 15, 50, 19, 13, 7, 40, and 42, respectively. Copyright © 1997 by the USCCB. All rights reserved. Used with permission.

The description of true ministry on page 21 and the statement in paragraph 4 on handout 1 are quoted from *A Vision of Youth Ministry,* by the USCCB (Washington, DC: USCCB, 1986), pages 10 and 6. Copyright © 1986 by the USCCB. All rights reserved. Used with permission.

The words of the interviewee in the Reflect sidebar on page 21 are quoted from, the research findings listed on page 22 are paraphrased from, the words of the three interviewees in the Reflect sidebar on page 23 are quoted from, the words of the interviewee in the Reflect sidebar on page 24 are quoted from, and the extracts from interviews on handout 34 are quoted from "Effective Youth Ministry Practices in Catholic Parishes," a joint research project of the Center for Ministry Development and Saint Mary's Press, in collaboration with the National Federation for Catholic Youth Ministry. The 2002 study is published in *Effective Practices for Dynamic Youth Ministry,* by Thomas East et al. (Winona, MN: Saint Mary's Press, 2004). All rights reserved.

The words of Pope John Paul II on page 23 are quoted from "Thirty-second World Day of Prayer for Vocations" (1995), at *www.vatican.va/holy_father/john_paul_ii/messages/vocations/documents/hf_jp-ii_mes_18101994_world-day-for-vocations_en.html,* accessed May 13, 2003.

The words in "For Further Reflection" on pages 23–24 are adapted from *The Leadership Bible, New International Version,* by Dr. Sidney Buzzell and Bill Perkins (Grand Rapids, MI: Zondervan Publishing House, 1998), page 1204. Copyright © 1998 by Kenneth Boa, Sidney Buzzell, and William Perkins (notes). Used with permission of The Zondervan Corporation.

The prayer on page 24 is quoted from *Prayer for Parish Groups: Preparing and Leading Prayer for Group Meetings,* by Donal Harrington and Julie Kavanagh (Winona, MN: Saint Mary's Press, 1998), page 37. Copyright © 1998 by Donal Harrington and Julie Kavanagh. Used with permission of Columba Book Service.

The words of the Lord's Prayer on handout 7 are quoted from the English translation of the *Catechism of the Catholic Church* for use in the United States of America, number 2759. Copyright © 1994 by the United States Catholic Conference, Inc.—Libreria Editrice Vaticana.

The parents' words on handout 7 are used with permission of the author, Kathleen Kensinger of Ralston, Nebraska.

The prayer service on handout 11 is adapted from *Give Your Gifts: The Prayer Services,* by Linda M. Baltikas and Robert W. Piercy (Chicago: GIA Publications, 1999), pages 40–42. Copyright © 1999 by GIA Publications Inc., Chicago, IL. All rights reserved. Used with permission.

The celebrant's words on page 93 are quoted from the English translation of *The Rite of Baptism for Children* (New York: Catholic Book Publishing Co., 1985), pages 38 and 39. Copyright © 1969 by the International Commission on English in the Liturgy Inc. All rights reserved. Used with permission.

The material on resource 3 is adapted from *People Skills: How to Assert Yourself, Listen to Others, and Resolve Conflicts,* by Robert Bolton (New York: Simon and Schuster, 1979), pages 17–26. Copyright © 1979 by Simon and Schuster, Inc. Adapted with permission of Simon and Schuster Adult Publishing Group.

The prayer on handout 19 is from *Six Ways to Pray from Six Great Saints,* by Gloria Hutchinson [Cincinnati: Saint Anthony Messenger Press, 1982], page 24. Copyright © 1982 by Saint Anthony Messenger Press.

The statistics in step 10 on pages 150–151 and in step 2 of the activity "Reflective Listening Skills" on page 156 are from "Communication Without Words," by Albert Mehrabian, *Psychology Today,* September 1968, volume 2, number 4, page 53. Copyright © 1968 by Communications/Research/Machines.

The material on handout 29 and on the CD-ROM background piece is adapted from *Leadership for Life: Discovering Your Gifts for Christian Leadership,* by Michael Poulin, Lori Spanbauer, Joan Weber, and Jennifer Willems (Naugatuck, CT: Center for Ministry Development, 1997), pages 85–91 and 13–40. Copyright © 1997 by the Center for Ministry Development. Used with permission.

The material on handouts 30 and 32 is adapted from *Effective Meeting Skills— A Practical Guide for More Productive Meetings,* first edition, by Marion E. Haynes (Menlo Park, CA: Crisp Publications, 1988), pages 26–27 and 3. Copyright © 1988 by Crisp Publications. Used with permission of Course Techology, a division of Thomson Learning: *www.tomsonrights.com.* Fax 800-730-2215.

The words of Martin Luther King Jr. on the CD-ROM background piece are quoted from *I Have a Dream: Writings and Speeches that Changed the World* (San Francisco: HarperSanFrancisco, 1992), page 53. Copyright © 1986, 1992 by Coretta Scott King, executrix of the Estate of Martin Luther King Jr.

The dictionary definitions on the CD-ROM background piece are quoted from *Merriam-Webster's Collegiate Dictionary,* tenth edition.

To view copyright terms and conditions for Internet materials cited here, log on to the home pages for the referenced Web sites.

During this book's preparation, all citations, facts, figures, names, addresses, telephone numbers, Internet URLs, and other pieces of information cited within were verified for accuracy. The authors and Saint Mary's Press staff have made every attempt to reference current and valid sources, but we cannot guarantee the content of any source, and we are not responsible for any changes that may have occurred since our verification. If you find an error in, or have a question or concern about, any of the information or sources listed within, please contact Saint Mary's Press.